SUGGESTIONS IN DESIGN

EGYPTIAN ASSYRIAN GRECIAN EUROPEAN

UGGESTIONS IN DESIGN

THREE THOUSAND YEARS OF ORNAMENTS · STYLES · MOTIFS

More than 1000 original drawings
by John Leighton

With a new introduction
by Edward Lucie-Smith

PADDINGTON PRESS LTD

NEW YORK & LONDON

Library of Congress Cataloging in Publication Data

Leighton, John, 1822-1912.
　　Suggestions in design.

　　Reprint of the plates from the 1880 ed. published by
Blackie, London.
　　　1.　Design, Decorative.　2.　Decoration and ornament.
I.　Title.
NK1510.L493　1977　　745.4　　76-53617
ISBN 0-448-22615-4

Printed in England by Balding & Mansell Ltd., Wisbech, Cambs.
Cover designed by Colin Lewis

IN THE UNITED STATES
PADDINGTON PRESS LTD.
Distributed by
GROSSET & DUNLAP

IN THE UNITED KINGDOM
PADDINGTON PRESS LTD.

IN CANADA
Distributed by
RANDOM HOUSE OF CANADA LTD.

IN AUSTRALIA
Distributed by
ANGUS & ROBERTSON PTY. LTD.

Introduction

John Leighton's *Suggestions in Design* is a major but neglected source for the history of design in the second half of the nineteenth century. Leighton, who also used the pseudonym Luke Limner, was one of the most prolific British designers of the period. He was represented in the Great Exhibition of 1851, and showed his work in most of the great International Exhibitions that followed it. In 1878, he served as a member of the jury at the Paris Exhibition.

In its original form, which consisted of only 47 plates, *Suggestions in Design* was published in 1852–3. It was re-published in 1880, doubled in size, and this is the form in which it is now reproduced. The interest of this work lies not so much in its originality as in its comprehensiveness. It tells us what sources were available to late Victorian designers and how they made use of them. The Publishers' Preface prefixed to the second edition is careful to emphasize that these are all *original* designs. They are, it says, "conceived in the spirit and with the proper art feeling of the various styles to which they severally belong, and are the accumulated result of long and arduous studies. They are intended as aids to design rather than for servile imitation or direct appropriation, serving to represent the type of many designs and not the exact portraits of any."

The first thing that will perhaps strike anyone who looks at the book today is the very wide range of sources upon which Leighton was able to draw. His series of plates contains exercises in the Egyptian, Assyrian, Greek, Persian and Moorish manners, among others. This range of sources reveals in turn the wide range of late Victorian culture. In fact, by the time the second edition of the book came out, the art-historical pattern perceived by educated people already bore a close resemblance to the one that exists today. People were becoming aware of Palaeolithic art, though some major discoveries, such as Lascaux, remained to be made. The Assyrian excavations of Layard and Botta had caused great excitement as long ago as the 1840's, and more recently Schliemann had added a new chapter to the history of Greek civilization through his excavations at Mycenae.

There were, of course, things about the late nineteenth-century view of cultural history which seem strange to us today. Among them is its bias in favor of European art. Leighton's collection of examples is, for its time, relatively advanced because he includes just one plate which is based on ethnographical material. James Colling, who supplied the introduction to the 1881 edition, seems indeed to have been faintly discomfited by this piece of boldness. "Although there is an extreme rudeness in the forms used by savage tribes," he says apologetically, "yet there evidently is a meaning which runs through them, and there cannot be a doubt that many of them are of a highly symbolic character, had we but the power to read or interpret them." Colling does, however, grasp the point that much of the ornamentation to be found on these barbarous-looking ethnographical objects had a functional purpose—that the carving on the handle of a Maori war-club was intended to give the man who used it a better grip.

Maori and Aztec art seem, however, to have been the only products of primitive civilizations to have attracted Leighton, and nearly all his examples seem to be derived from these two sources. (Plate 1, figure 6, is particularly fascinating because it seems to anticipate the early work of Jacob Epstein, still several decades away.) One reason why Leighton was attracted to these two cultures in particular may be that they were well represented in accessible publications—for example, in the lavishly illustrated books devoted to the voyages of Captain Cook, and in Catherwood's *Views of ancient monuments in Central America, Chiapas and Yucatan*, published in 1841. By contrast, not the slightest attention is paid to the art of Africa which was to arouse such excitement among the founders of the Modern Movement.

If Leighton is advanced for his day in his treatment of "primitive" source-material, he is old-fashioned by our standards in his attitude towards the products of the Early Middle Ages. Under the general heading "Byzantine" he lumps together not only the art of Byzantium itself, but Romanesque, Celtic and Viking. However, the stylistic muddleheadedness of some of Leighton's ideas is less interesting than the way in which they forshadow the decorative fashions of the eighties and nineties. Plate 32, figure 4 supplies us with a pair of peacocks which indicate a clear link to the Aesthetic Movement; Plate 34, figure 7, is a small panel of interlace which seems to anticipate some of the ornamentation of Liberty Cymric silver and Tudric pewter.

While these designs display a certain degree of originality, the most genuinely original aspect of the collection is reflected in Leighton's advocacy of the Japanese decorative arts. This had been an interest of his from a very early period. He delivered a "Discourse on Japanese Art" at the Royal Institution as early as 1863. In the 1880's, Japan was to become the fountainhead of everything that was fashionable in the interior decoration and in the domestic objects of the day. The patterns Leighton gives are close to those which were used for the decoration of metalwork by leading silversmiths, among them, in England, the well-known Birmingham firm of Elkington & Co.

Yet it would be a mistake to be carried away by these moments of originality into thinking of *Suggestions in Design* as a pioneering work. It is valuable because it reflects a spectrum of possibilities, and thus enables us to gauge the state of play in design-thinking at the time when it was published. Leighton was not a pioneer in his own right, like his contemporary Christopher Dresser. He lays no claim to the place which Dresser has recently been given as a founder of contemporary theory of industrial design. It is worth comparing *Suggestions in Design* with Dresser's more modestly produced *Principles of Decorative Design*, which was issued in 1873. Dresser, too, believes that the designer must have an awareness and knowledge of the styles of the past, and must apply that knowledge to the materials he uses: "Men of the lowest degree of intelligence can dig clay, iron, or copper, or quarry stone: but these materials, if bearing the impress of mind, are ennobled and rendered valuable, and the more strongly the material is marked with this ennobling impress the more valuable it becomes."

What Dresser is doing here is carrying on the moralizing tradition of John Ruskin, which made so deep an impression the whole Victorian aesthetic. It was Ruskin who concluded, in his *Lectures on Architecture and Painting*, that glass and iron would never become important materials in architecture because this would not be in accordance with the Bible: "The force of the image of the Corner Stone, as used throughout Scripture, would completely be lost, if the Christian and civilized world were ever extensively to employ any other material than earth and rock in their domestic buildings . . ." Dresser is not inhibited by this kind of contorted Evangelical theology from seizing upon what is technically innovative, and trying to put it to its best use, but he still has the idea that there is a kind of morality inherent in materials. "It is strange but true," he remarks sadly, "that the worker in one material seems rarely to be satisfied with making his works look as well and consistent as possible; he desires rather to form poor imitations of something else." Ruskin's ideas are thus caught in the process of being transformed into the rational tenets of Bauhaus design— what is moral, in the form and ornamentation of both architecture and objects of everyday use, thus insensibly becomes what is rational.

Suggestions in Design does not, as Dresser's book does, constantly revert to the principle of logic of construction and fitness for use—though Colling, as Leighton's spokesman and alter ego, occasionally pays lip service to principles that both Christopher Dresser and William Morris would have approved. Curved legs on both tables and chairs are condemned because they lead to structural weakness; the reader is told that "stability of construction should be apparent as well as real," and is adjured to "avoid shams both in construction and ornament". But one feels that these warnings are inserted in deference to the intellectual climate of the time, rather than because those who used Leighton's work as a source were going to pay much attention to them.

A more important aspect of Leighton's guiding design attitude is expressed by Colling when he remarks that "natural forms, plants, animals and the like, cannot be rendered literally for purposes or ornament, but require to be treated in a conventional manner." This runs contrary to Ruskin's conviction that the proper ornament for buildings was a representation of the "birds and flowers which are singing and budding in the fields around them." But we must remember, of course, that Ruskin was only a gifted amateur, while Leighton's ideas had been built up over years of professional practice. He realized, even if unconsciously, that however close to nature a particular motif might seem to the untutored eye, it had inevitably been subject to processes of organization before it could be put to use. Nevertheless, Colling's statement, when contrasted with Ruskin's, calls our attention to one important but little-noticed characteristic of the complex interplay of ornamental styles during the nineteenth century—the battle between extreme naturalism and conventionalized pattern.

Naturalism itself is not confined to any particular period. It is visible in much of the work of the 1850s, and visible again at the end of the century in certain types of Art Nouveau. In some fields of design—metalwork is one of them—it was encouraged by the invention of new technical processes such as electrotyping, which made it easy to reproduce the most complex natural forms directly. The periodical *Art Union* spoke enthusiastically, in 1848, of the possibilities offered by this process: "We are enabled to give a permanent metallic form to the most elaborately fashioned flowers of nature—to preserve every leaf with all its delicate venations and even its downy covering—to sheath the gossamer wings of the dragonfly, or the most fragile moth, in gold and silver, without altering their geometric outline; and indeed to secure the perfection and the delicacy of Nature's most lovely or more fantastic creations in all the permanence of metallic solidity." Electrotyping, like photography, suggested to the lay mind that the creative artist could be made superfluous. The perfection of the natural world—perfect because divinely created—could be given the means to record its own beauty.

Some of the most interesting plates in Leighton's collection are therefore those which are devoted to geometric patterns and to the conventionalizing of natural motifs. The "Floral Sprigs" of Plates 74–81 are especially fascinating. These seem predominantly formal—certainly more formal than similar designs produced by Morris & Co. Yet naturalism, though unbidden, keeps slyly reappearing —a good example is the pair of pea-pods, in Plate 80, figure 8.

The floral sprigs are also interesting for the extent to which they seem to find their inspiration in Eastern, and particularly Indian sources. Throughout the post-Renaissance period the European visual arts have adhered to a double standard. Not only has a distinction been drawn between the fine and the applied arts; but it is the applied arts which have been more open to exotic influences. Thus the eighteenth-century Meissen porcelain factory made the most perfect copies of the Japanese Kakiemon porcelains which were then so admired in Europe; and there have, in addition, been endless European imitations of such things as Chinese wallpapers and oriental lacquer. In French eighteenth-century furniture we sometimes find a mixture of Oriental and European lacquer panels used in the same piece.

At the same time that they used and imitated various Eastern sources, European designers also had a penchant for making a playful paraphrase of what was exotic. The *chinoiseries* and *turqueries* beloved of the eighteenth century supply a striking example of this. With the coming of the Neo-classical movement, things began to change, and we begin to find traces of the desire for correct archaeological reconstruction. It was not merely that potters like Josiah Wedgwood endeavored to produce convincing copies (in different material) of famous antiquities such as the Portland Vase. People genuinely began to feel an aversion for what they regarded as bastard styles. The place where this development can most easily be traced is the Gothic Revival.

At its beginnings, in the mid-eighteenth century, Gothic Revival was as much a matter of playful paraphrase as exercises in mock-Chinese or mock-Turkish manner. In his first flush of enthusiasm for his new villa Strawberry Hill, Horace Walpole spoke of it as a "plaything house." Gradually, interest became more serious: the great architects of the Victorian age were undoubtedly considerable scholars where the Gothic was concerned, and, when engaged in designing buildings which had the same function as their mediæval predecessors, particularly churches, could provide pastiche which was both convincing and formally coherent. Their difficulties arose from the practical point of view, when they were asked to produce in the mediæval manner something for which there was no direct mediæval precedent, such as an office building or a luxury hotel; or when they had to meet demands for a degree of contemporary convenience, as in their designs for country houses. But to do them justice, they did not really think that these difficulties were difficulties at all. Though they took the Gothic, and indeed the other revivalist styles in which they sometimes worked, perfectly seriously, they were not content merely to imitate. They thought of the styles they used as a grammar which could be used to say anything they liked.

If this is true of Victorian architects, it is doubly true of Victorian designers. As one looks through the pages of *Suggestions in Design*, one is struck, not only by the very wide stylistic range, but by the comparatively unspecific nature of many of the ideas. It is only occasionally—the Gothic keyplate, Plate 39, figure 13, is an instance—that one finds a design which is suitable only for one purpose.

Leighton's idea was clearly that the good professional would be accustomed to manipulating all kinds of ornamental motifs, and would know how to adapt them to serve very different practical functions.

The extreme eclecticism of Leighton's taste does, however, prompt another rather different series of reflections. As I have already suggested at the beginning of this essay, the 101 plates collected here demonstrate beyond possibility of argument that the historical and geographical schema we now use to make sense of what we know concerning the visual arts was in most respects complete by the time the book was published. The great change is that no modern designer would dare follow Leighton's attempt to absorb such a mass of material, and put his own imprint on it, even if he believed in the necessity of this type of historicism. Leighton stands at the beginning of an age of specialization, but has not yet fallen to its demands. He feels free to make use of the whole area of knowledge which is open to him.

The ultimately fascinating thing about *Suggestions in Design*, if we regard it as something more than a source-book, is to trace this effort of one mind and one talent to deal with such a heterogeneous collection of forms and ideas in a way that makes them uniquely his own. It is easy enough to find things among the plates which are recognizably "Victorian," using the adjective in rather a crudely ironic way. The age which put ruffles around the piano-legs because it considered the sight of them improper was certainly going to insist that the Atlantes based on those which form part of the ancient Greek temple as Agrigentum (Plate 7, figures 5 and 6) should be decently draped before they were offered for contemporary use. Yet, in general, the book calls into question any over-simplified view of Victorian style.

For example, some of the designs look back to the very beginning of the reign while others— chiefly in the Renaissance section—turn out to be related to what progressive architects like Norman Shaw were producing at the moment when the volume came out.

In order to arrive at an understanding of the forces which created both Leighton and his book, we have to yield to a paradox, which is that in a work devoted to the exploration of styles of ornament, the notion of style is redundant. The collection of plates is based on the assumption that the professional designer is in control of any mode within which he chooses to exercise his invention and his talent. It is not too far-fetched, I think, to say that this in some ways resembles the colonial situation of the same period, where the Englishman clearly felt he was qualified to rule any people, and to control any society, no matter how great the disparity of cultural background.

The price the professional designer is asked to pay, in the circumstances I have outlined, is lack of contact with the actual work. Though there are things in *Suggestions in Design* which seem to anticipate the aesthetic of the Arts and Crafts Movement, the fundamental difference is certainly the lack of physical contact between the creator and his product. Colling's introduction contains no word about the importance of hand work, and in a broad sense we can take it that this book represents precisely the approach which the supporters of the Arts and Crafts Movement were to revolt against. Though there are, in the notes to the plates, occasional suggestions for an appropriate material in which the design could be carried out, and though there are indeed a whole series of designs under the heading "Metal Work," there is no suggestion that the actual stuff from which the object is made should govern the form it takes when it is finished.

Dresser, though he is sometimes spoken of as an Arts and Crafts designer, is also a man who stands at a distance from the cult of the handmade. But he too, as I have already said, shows a wide divergence of aim from Leighton. He is a man who tries to find the point at which the logic of process and the logic of use coincide, and it is this, above everything, which gives him his place as the first modern industrial designer. Leighton, though strictly speaking he is Dresser's contemporary, for all practical purposes belongs to a different and earlier epoch.

The most fruitful comparison which can be made is not that between Leighton and those who were to follow him, but between him and the influential designers of an earlier epoch. Despite evident differences of practical aim, there is a similarity between *Suggestions in Design* and the books issued in the preceding century by Chippendale and Sheraton. The two cabinet-makers aimed to instruct the public and to educate their professional colleagues; at the same time, they aimed to educate taste—that is, to make it sympathetic to themselves and to the ideas they were putting forward. The eclecticism which Leighton shows in such full and overflowing measure was already present in the suggestions put forward by the great furniture-designers of an earlier epoch. It is in them as much as in *Suggestions in Design* that we find expressed, though usually by implication, the notion that style was a question of choice, that there was no barrier to the embodiment of the whim of the individual.

This collection of plates is therefore almost the last flowering of a tradition which had its origins in the sixteenth century. Pattern-books such as that of Meissonier (which gave tremendous impetus to the growth of the Rococo in France) were one of the means whereby talented artists advertised their own gifts, and at the same time made propaganda for stylistic innovation. Leighton still has a kind of confidence in himself which he shares with these predecessors, but not with those who were to come after him. In his case, the confidence is based on the feeling that man had now reached a kind of plateau in his knowledge and understanding of the arts, and that he could thus feel confident of his own superiority over previous generations, simply through the sheer multiplicity of the choices which were now open to him. Man's ability to make those choices was not yet in question.

The reaction against this detached and Olympian view of man's relationship to his cultural heritage was bound to take place, and indeed it was already gathering momentum when Leighton's work was published. William Morris and Philip Webb had produced a considerable stock of designs which had nothing to do with the notion of imposed style which plays so important a role in Leighton's work. (This applies particularly to some of the glass and metalwork for which Webb was responsible in the late fifties and the early sixties, but it is also applicable to furniture—for instance to the versions of traditional Sussex chairs which were being made by Morris, Marshall, Faulkner & Co. in the seventies, and which have survived in quantities which prove their popularity at the time they were made.) We find no trace in Leighton of the notion of vernacular tradition, though he includes some instances of what he calls Elizabethan and Jacobean ornament. The concept of the vernacular gave a new gloss to the reliance on tradition which the nineteenth century was not yet willing to surrender. It led the aspiring designer to think of the spirit in which a thing was made before he considered its form and certainly before he considered how it was to be ornamented. This, in turn, though by very gradual stages, led to a concentration on the idea of process—the object, in its finished form, must visibly embody the processes which had been used to produce it. While the emphasis on process seemed at first to confirm the superiority of handwork to what was done by the machine, it led eventually to the thought that the machine also imposed its own grammar of forms. This, in turn, led directly to the kind of machine-design we now think of as typically modern, though there has recently been a growing realization that many so-called "necessities" in the forms of machine-made objects are nevertheless an unconscious expression of stylistic mannerism.

At the same time when the range of stylistic choices seems once again to be broadening, and when the spirit of nostalgia is making itself felt in every aspect of domestic design, Leighton's work acquires a new relevance. There is already a strong contemporary interest both in the Aesthetic Movement and in the Arts and Crafts revival, but we cannot understand either of these fully unless we know something of the background against which they arose.

Suggestions in Design offers a very full view of that background, and at the same time makes available once again the work of a man who is fully representative of some of the outstanding strengths and weaknesses of High Victorian culture.

Edward Lucie-Smith.

TRIBUS SAUVAGES. # SAVAGE TRIBES. WILDE STÄMME.

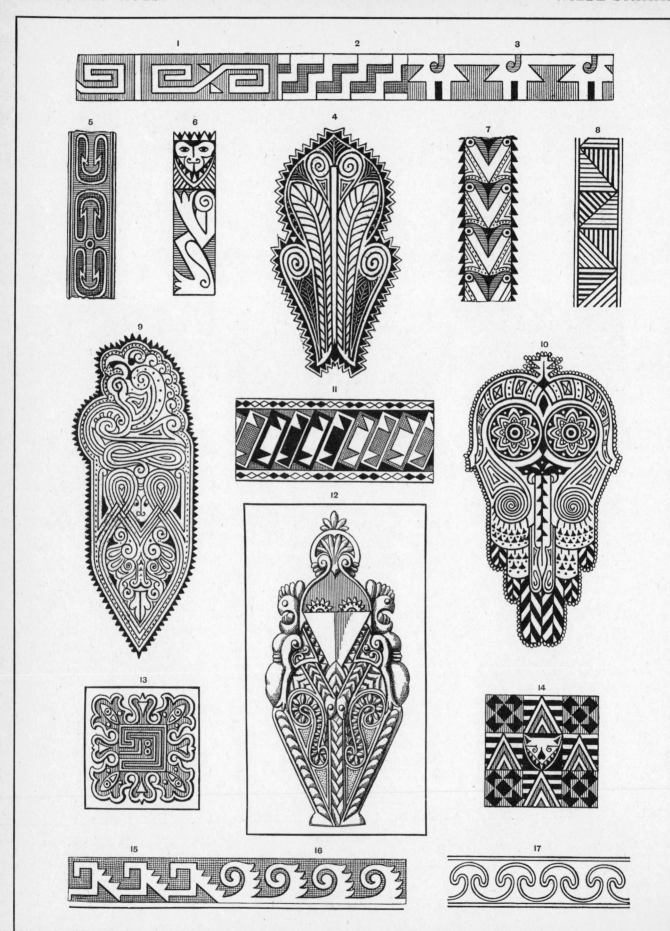

SUGGESTIONS IN DESIGN

BY JOHN LEIGHTON, F.S.A.

2.
EGYPTIAN.

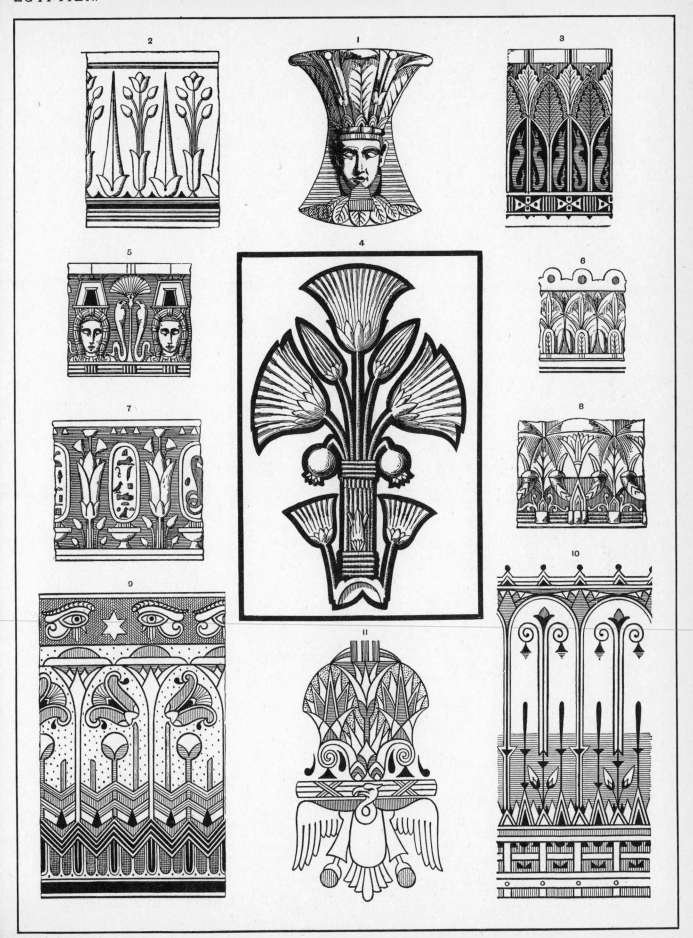

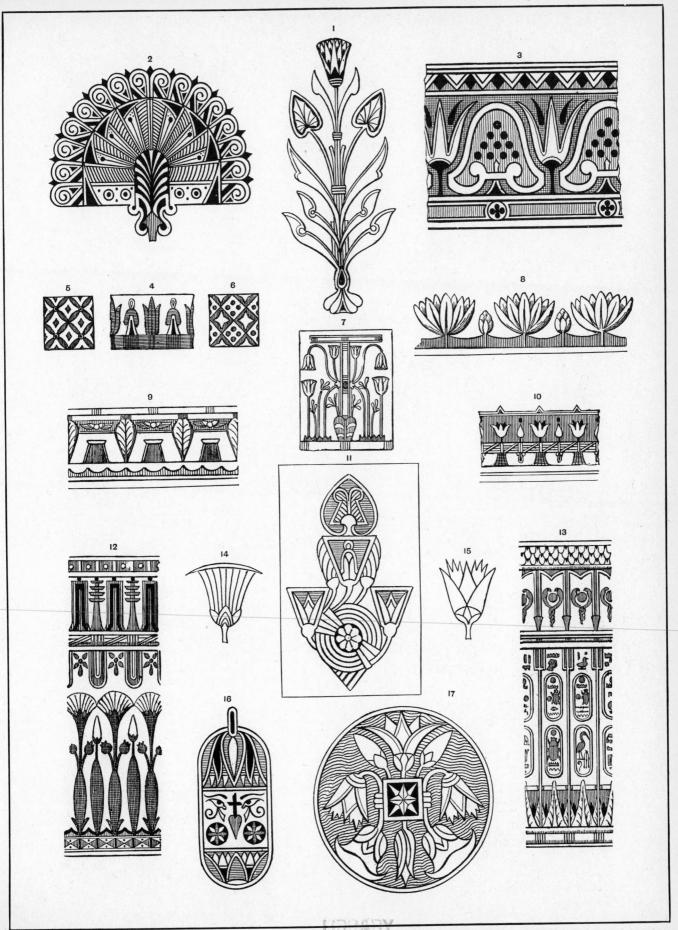

ASSYRIEN.   ASSYRIAN.   ASSYRISCH.

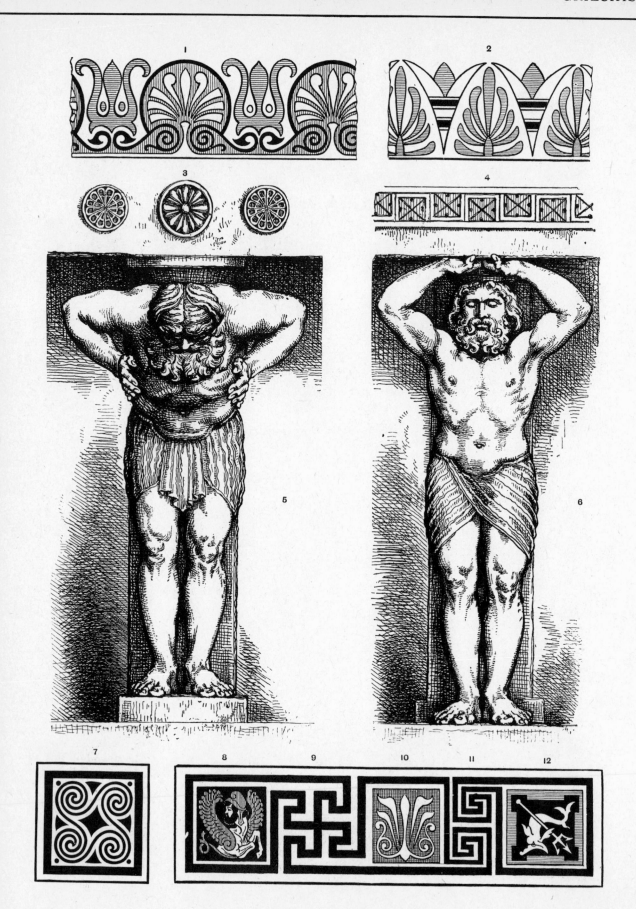

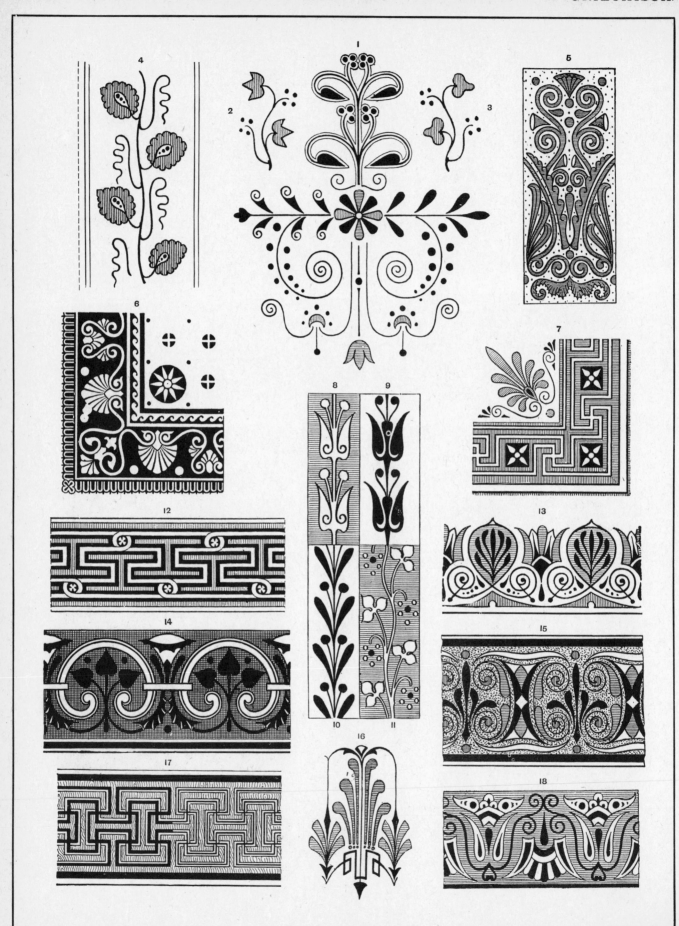

GREC ET ETRUSQUE.　　GREEK & ETRUSCAN.　　GRIECHISCH U. ETRUSKISCH.

POMPÉIEN.

POMPEIAN.

POMPEJISCH.

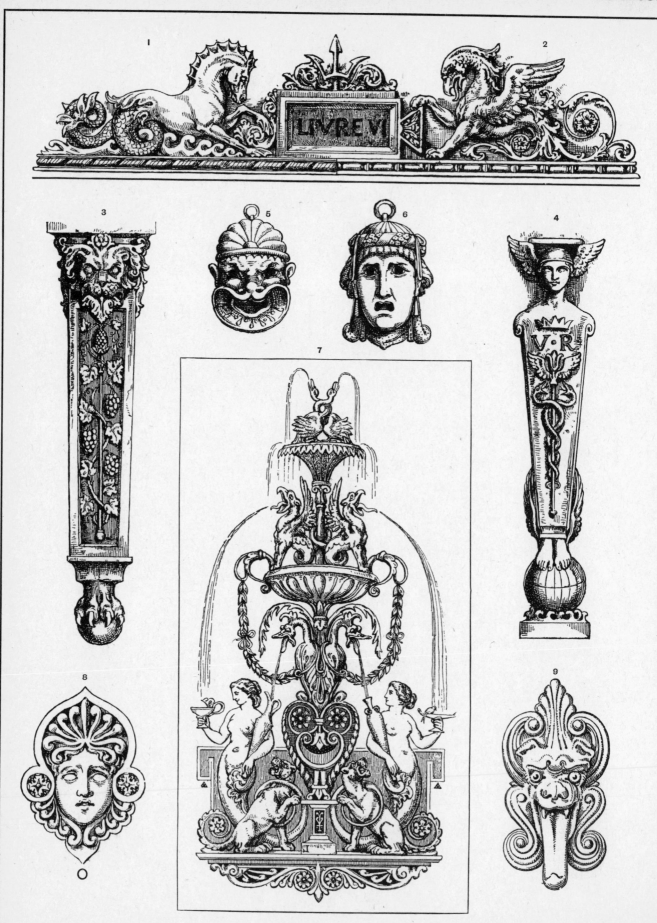

LIVRE VI

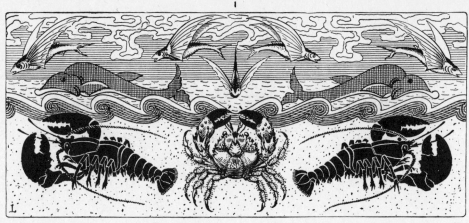

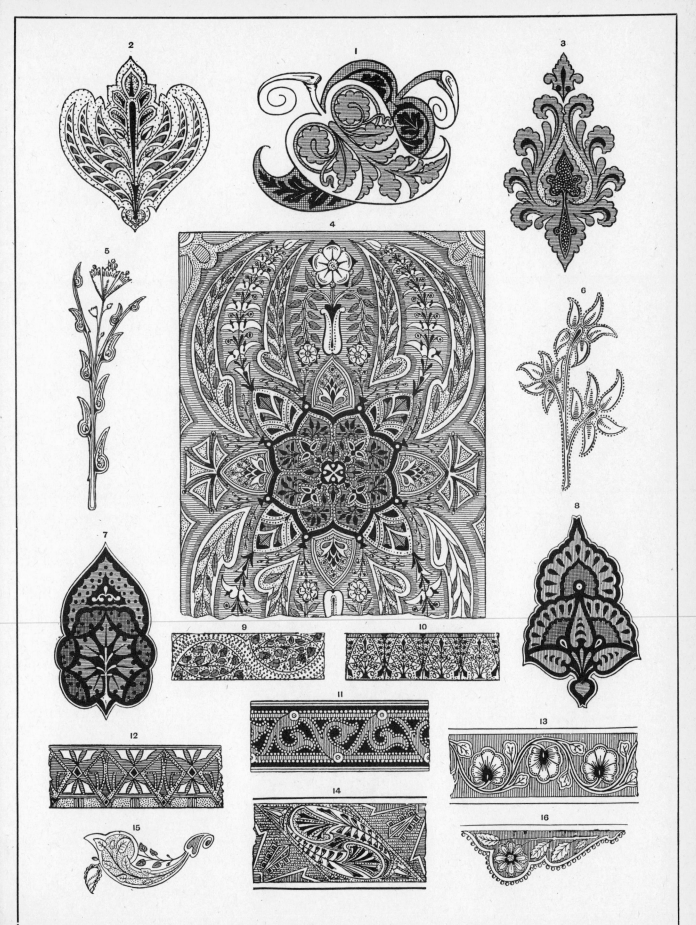

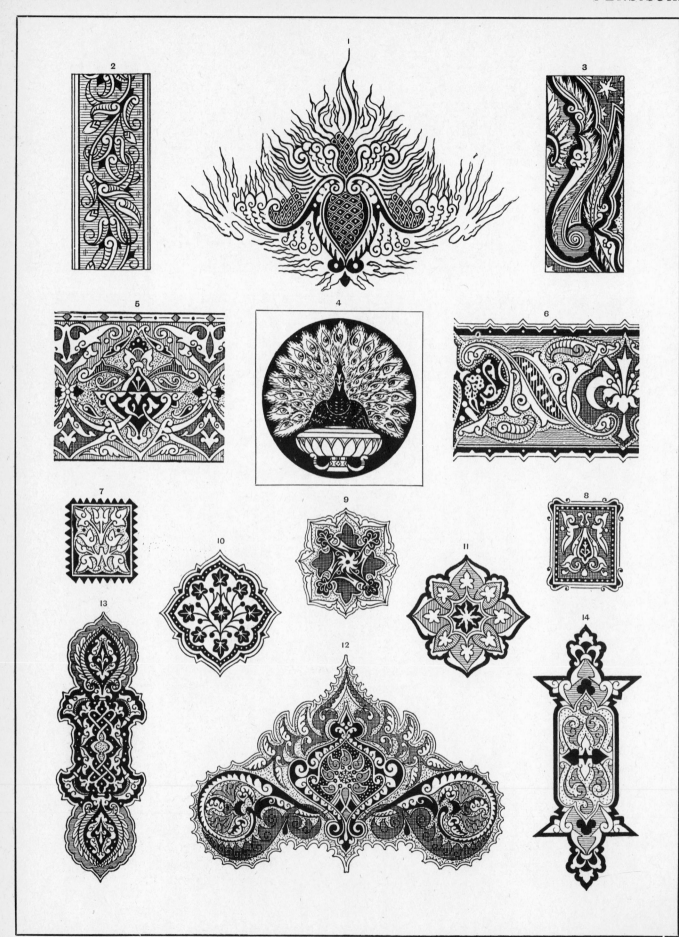

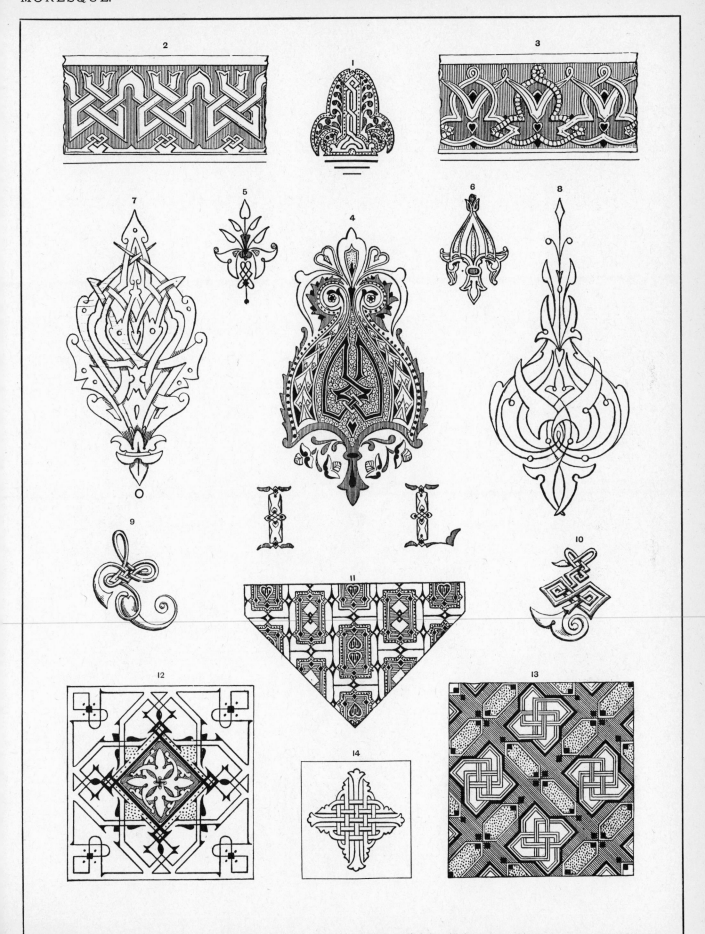

MORESQUE. MOORISH. MOHRISCH.

BYZANTIN.   # BYZANTINE.   BYZANTINISCH.

BYZANTINE.

MARK. LUKE. JOHN. MATTHEW.

BY JOHN LEIGHTON, F.S.A.

GOTHIQUE.

GOTHIC.

GOTHISCH.

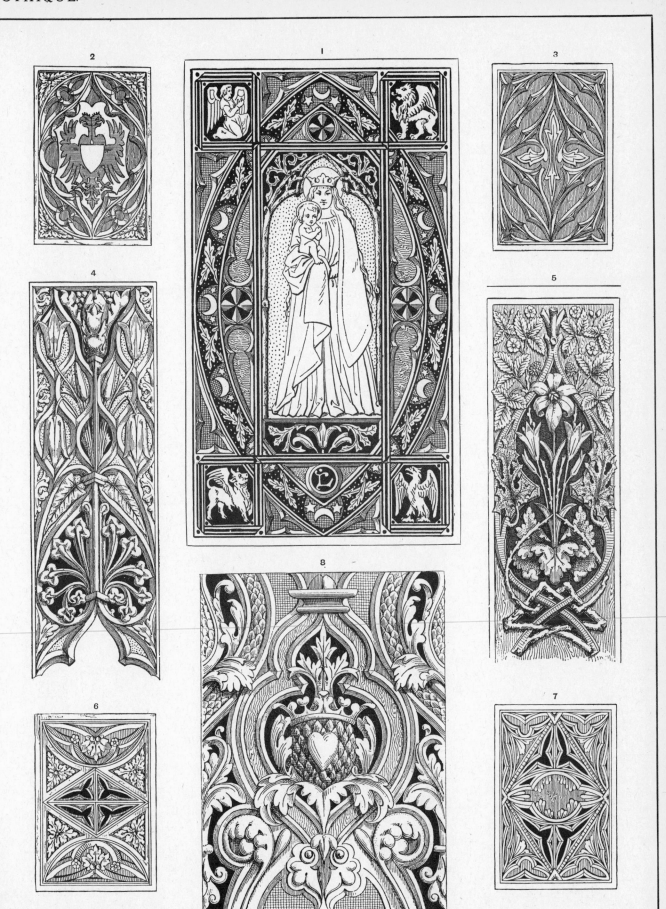

BY JOHN LEIGHTON, F.S.A.

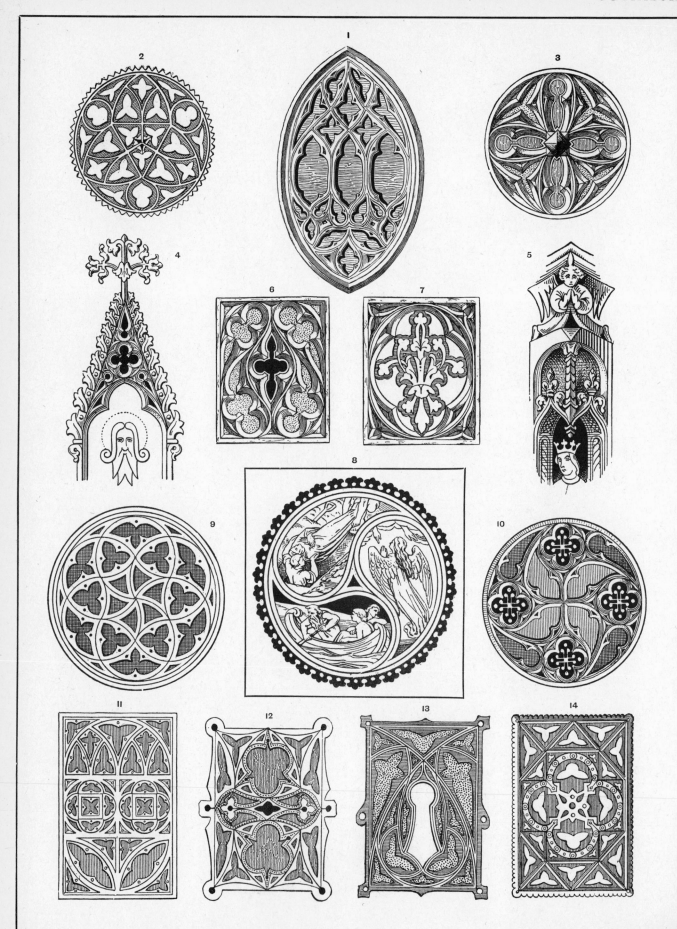

SUGGESTIONS IN DESIGN   BY JOHN LEIGHTON, F.S.A.

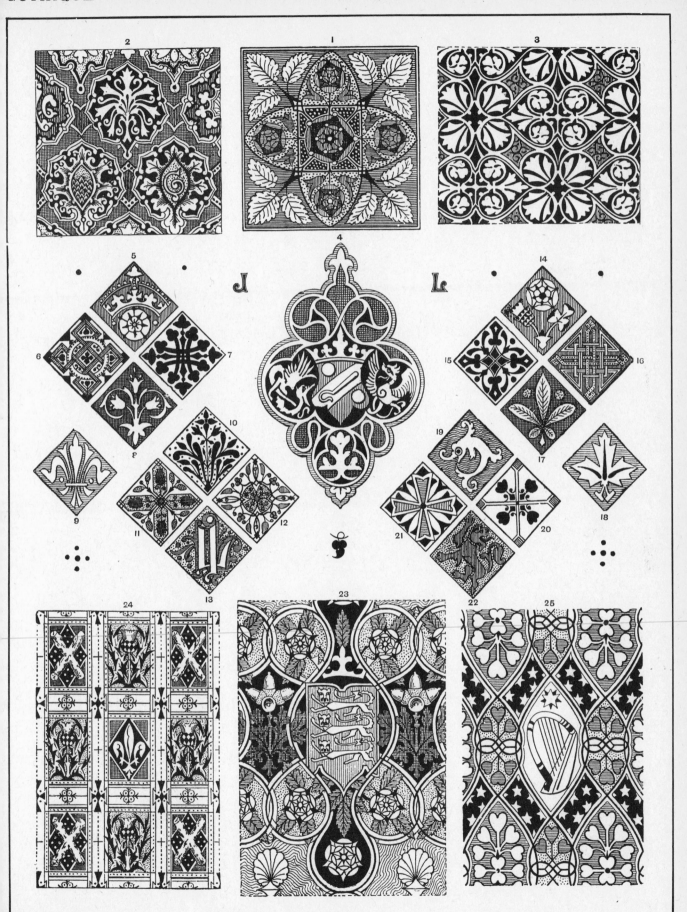

OUVRAGES METALLIQUES. METAL WORK. METALLISCHE WERKE.

GEOMETRIQUE.   GEOMETRIC.   GEOMETRISCH.

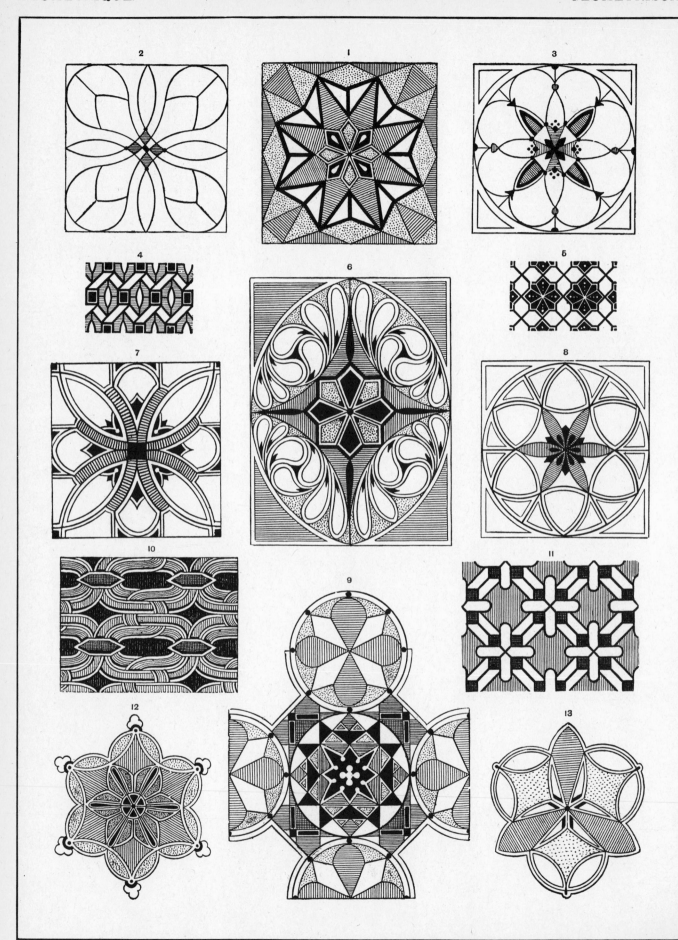

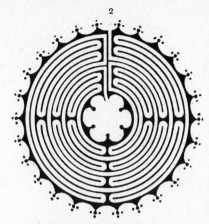

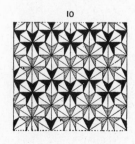

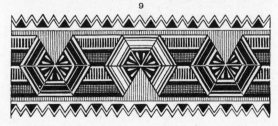

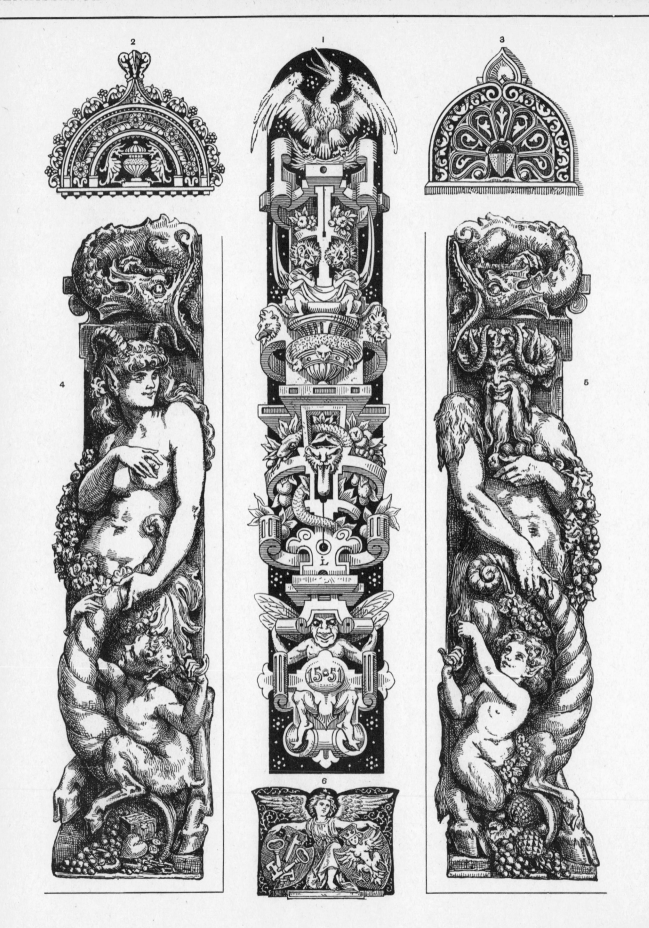

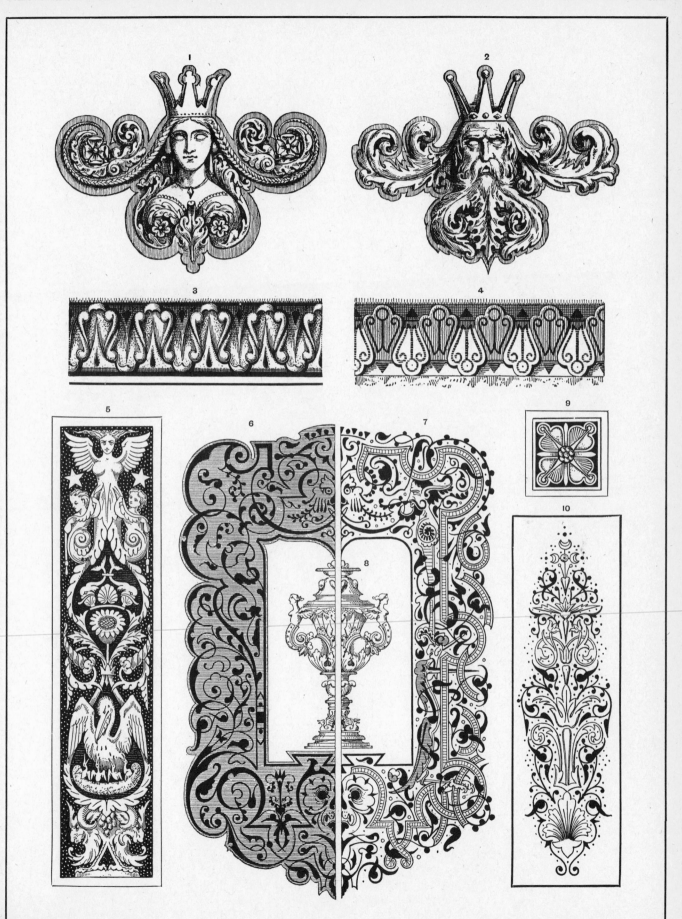

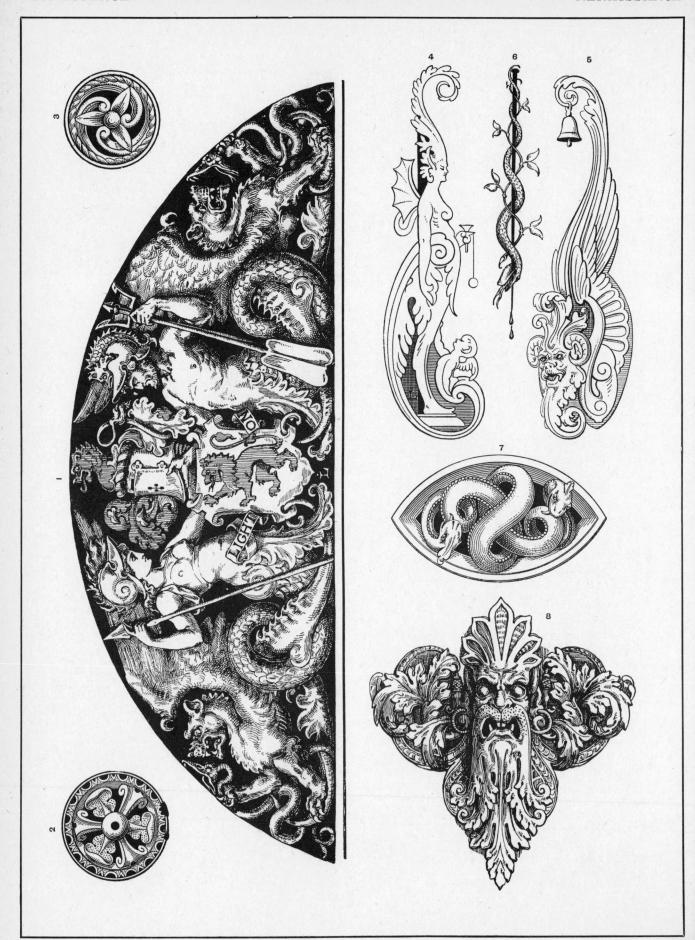

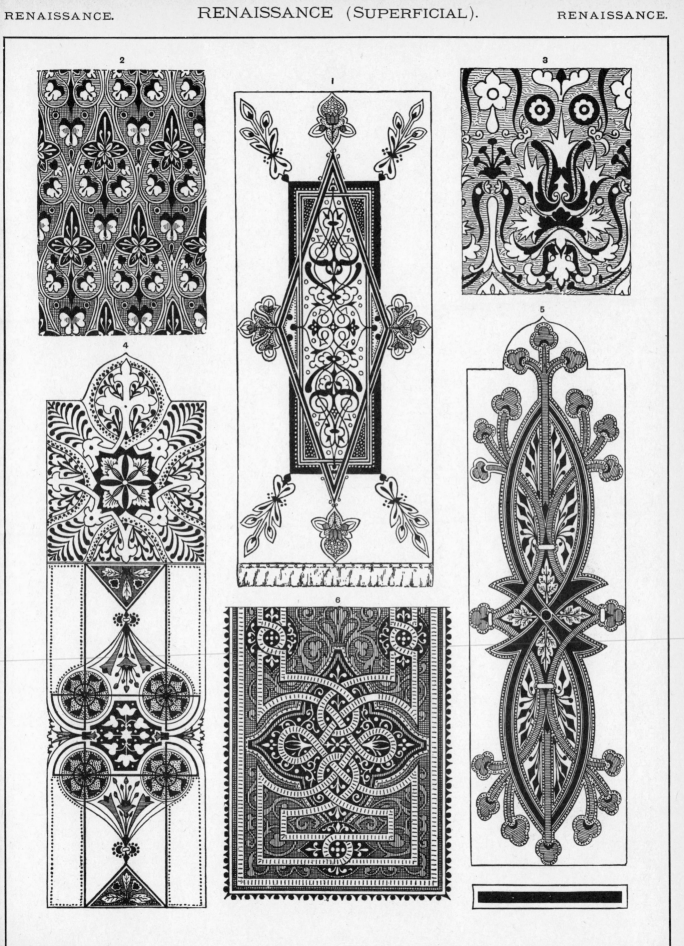

RENAISSANCE.   # RENAISSANCE (SUPERFICIAL).   RENAISSANCE.

RENAISSANCE.
(LOUIS XIV. AND LOUIS XV.)

BRINS FLORAUX. FLORAL SPRIGS. BLÜTHENZWEIGLEIN.

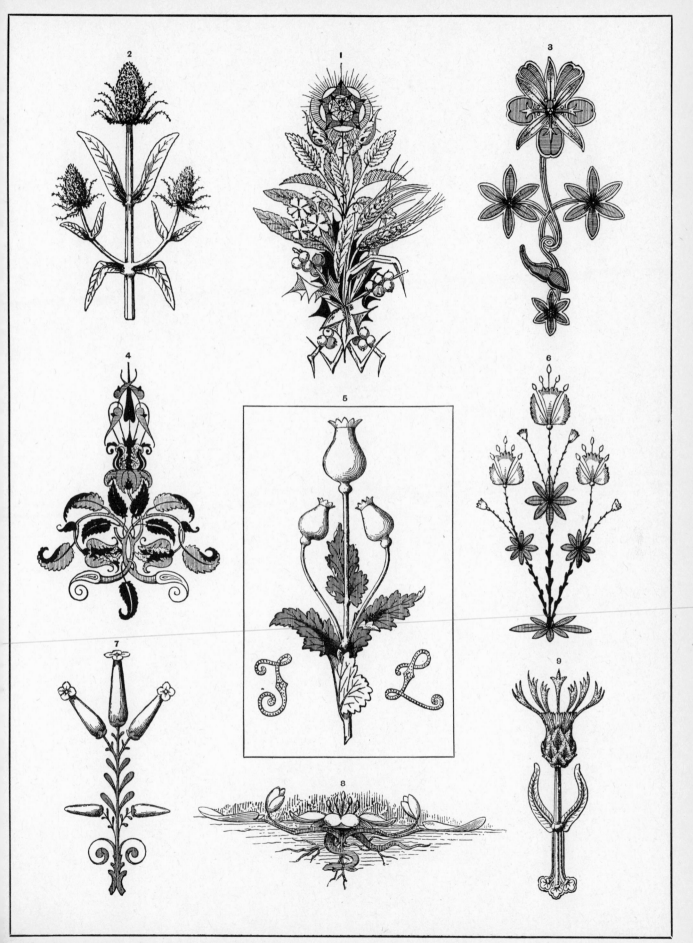

BRINS FLORAUX.   FLORAL SPRIGS.   BLÜTHENZWEIGLEIN.

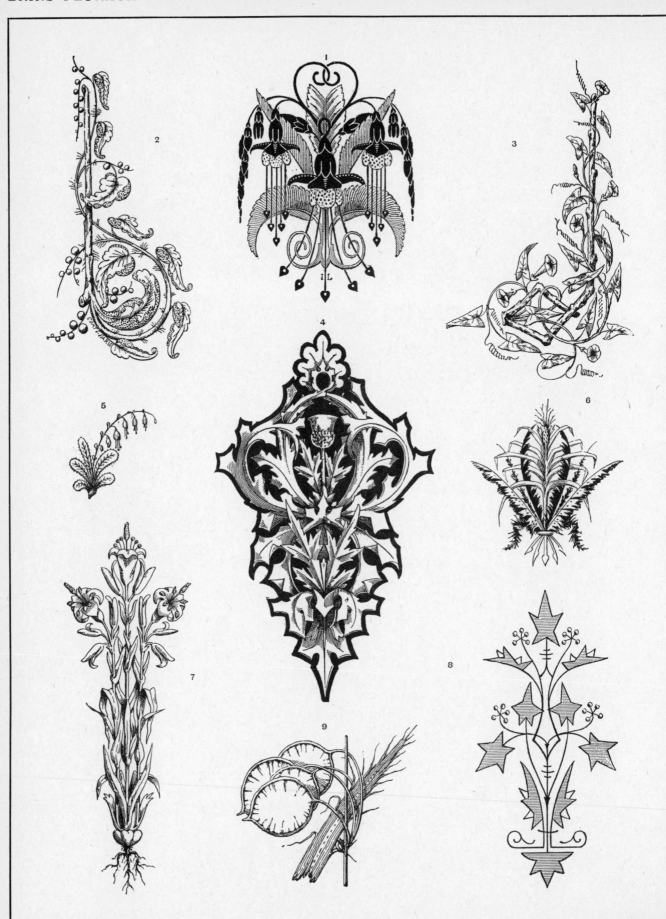

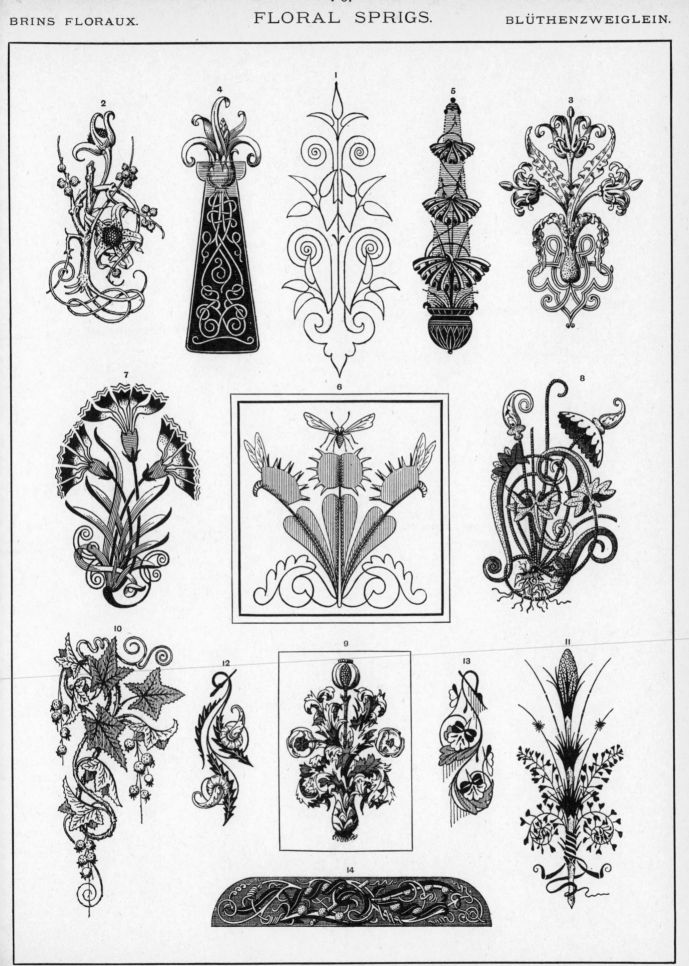

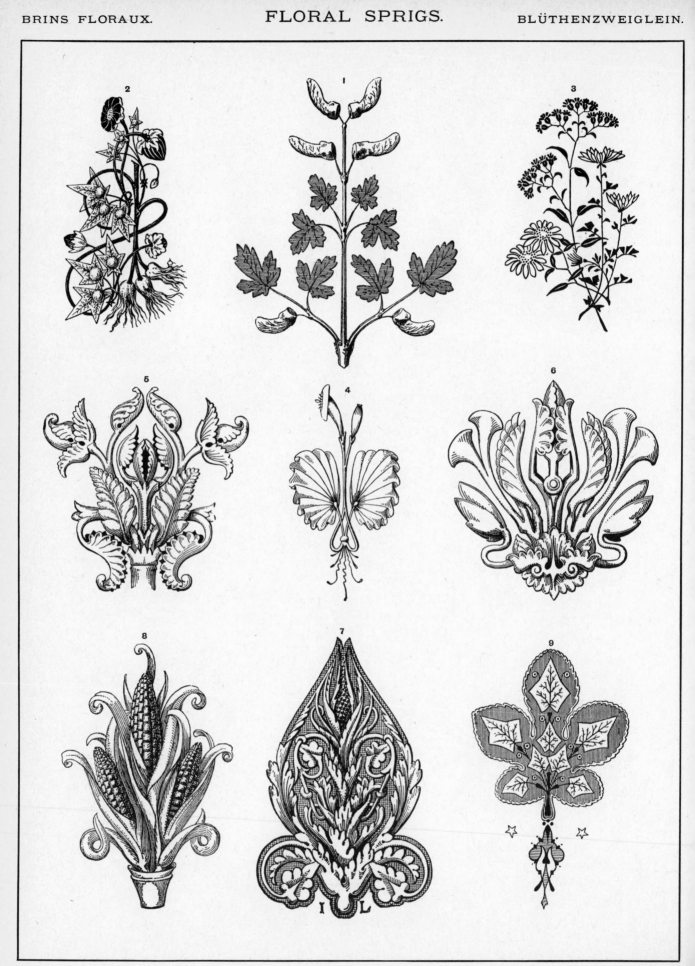

FLORAL SPRIGS.

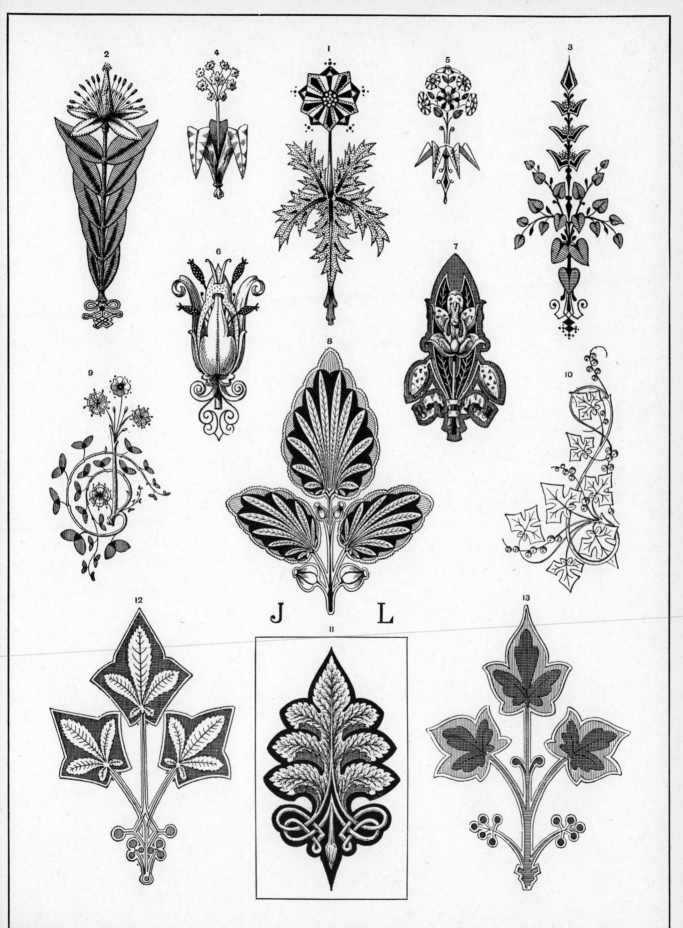

J L

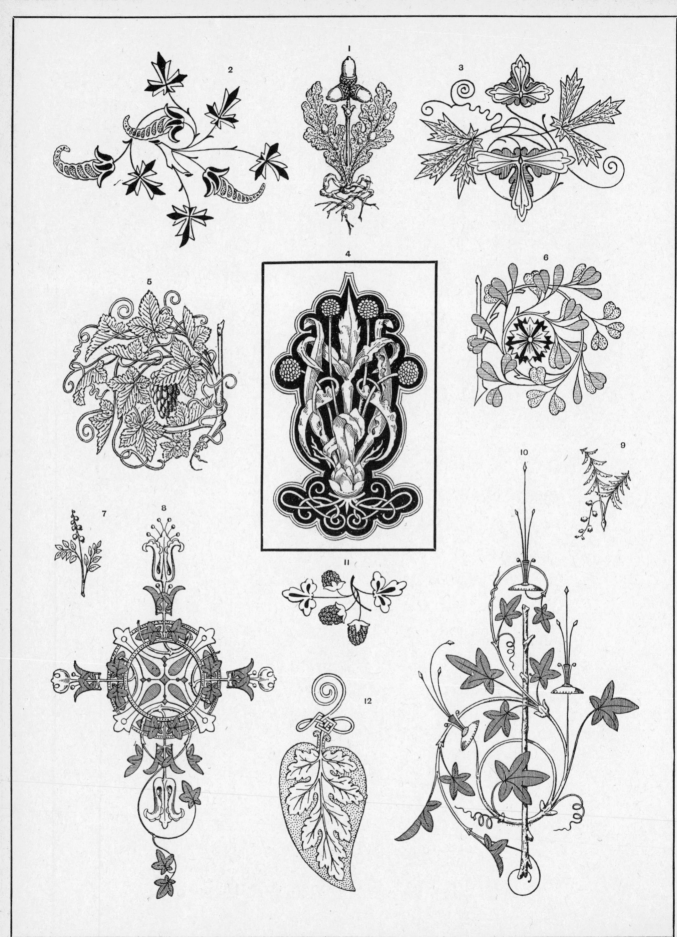

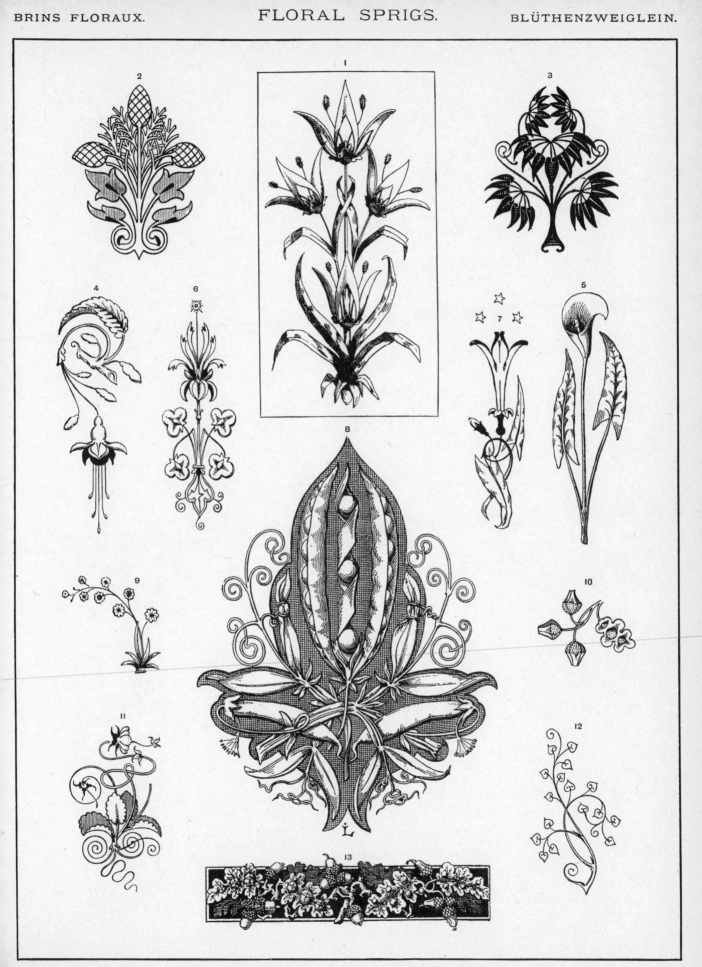

2

Matin.   MORNING.   Morgen.

3

Midi.   NOON.   Mittag.

1

NOCTV DIVQVE.   NOCTE NOCTV.

4

Soir.   EVENING.   Abend.

5

Nuit.   NIGHT.   Nacht.

J · L

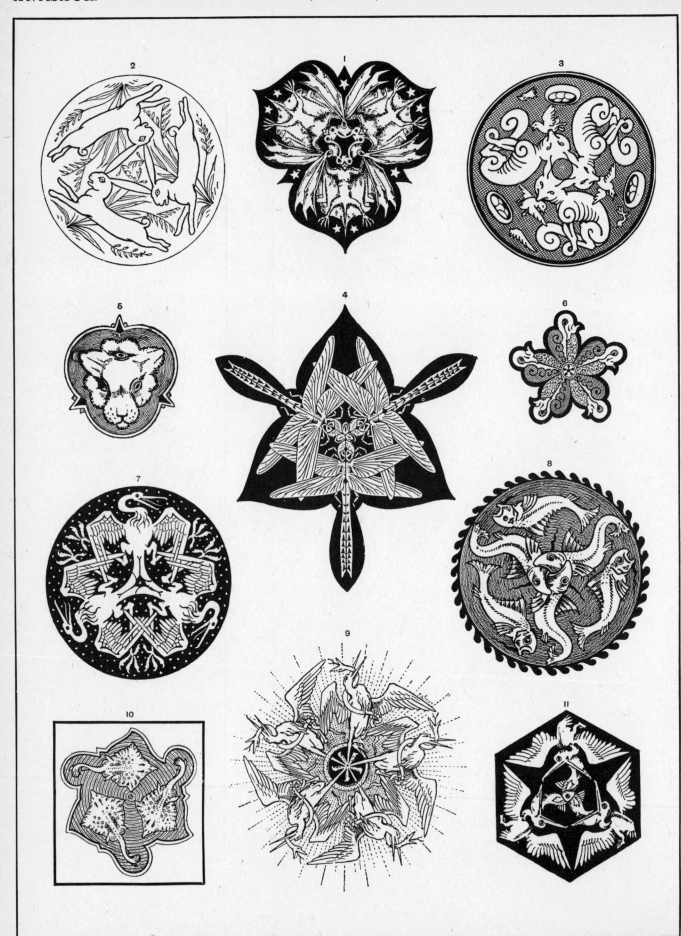

BY JOHN LEIGHTON, F.S.A.

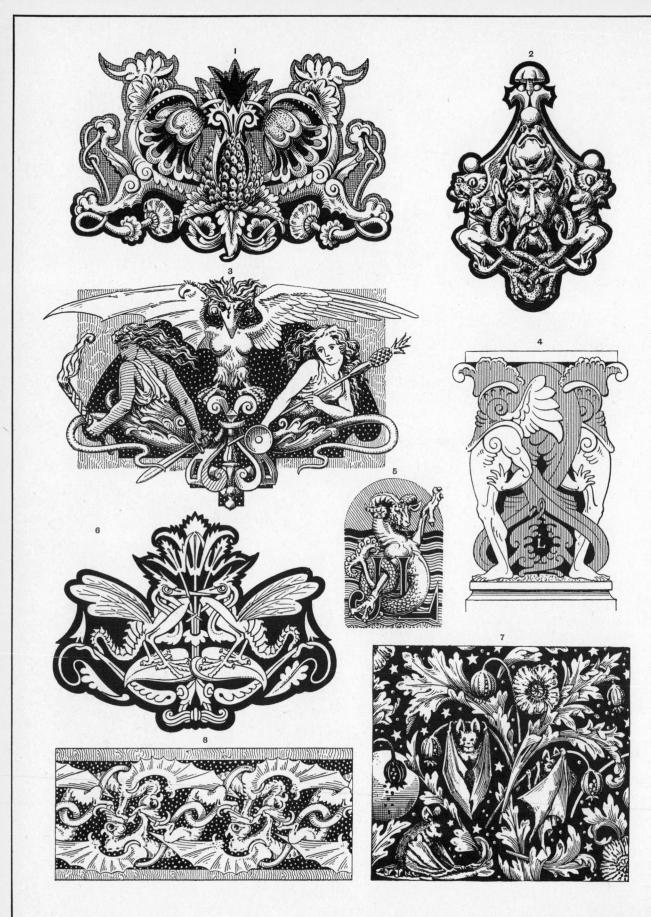

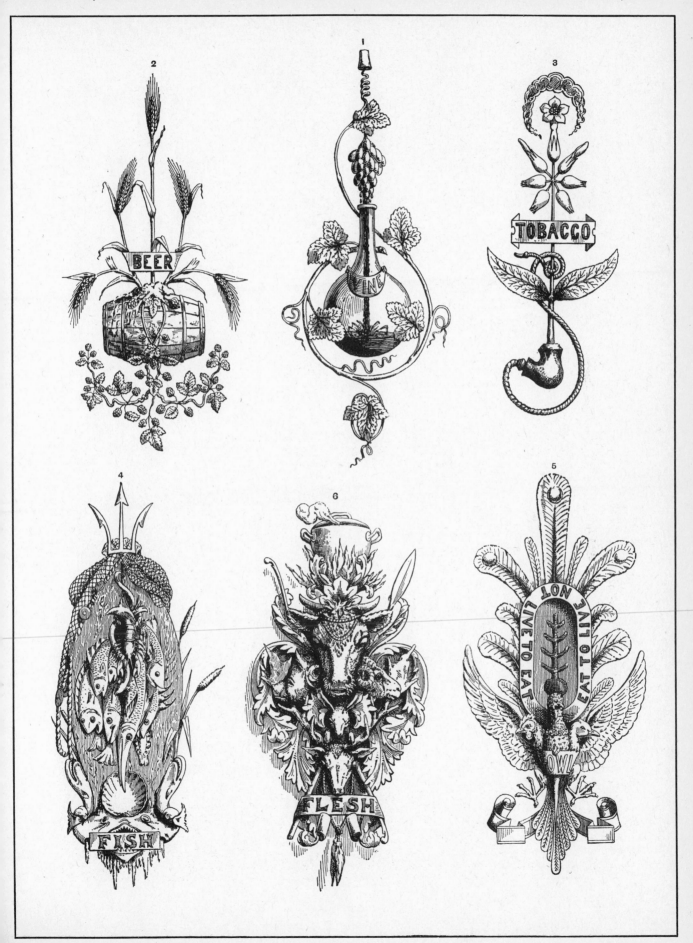

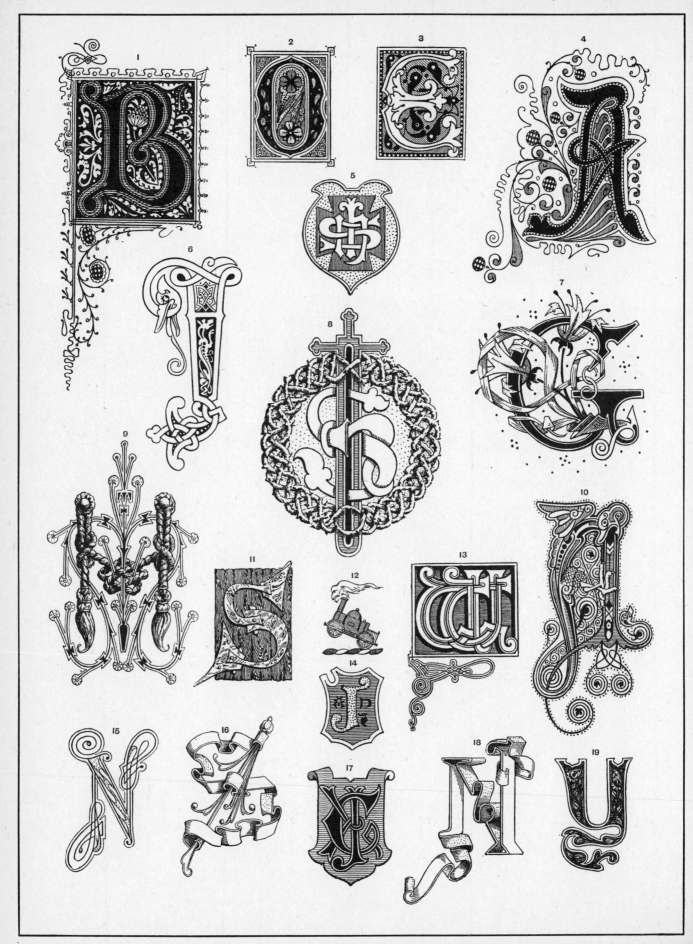

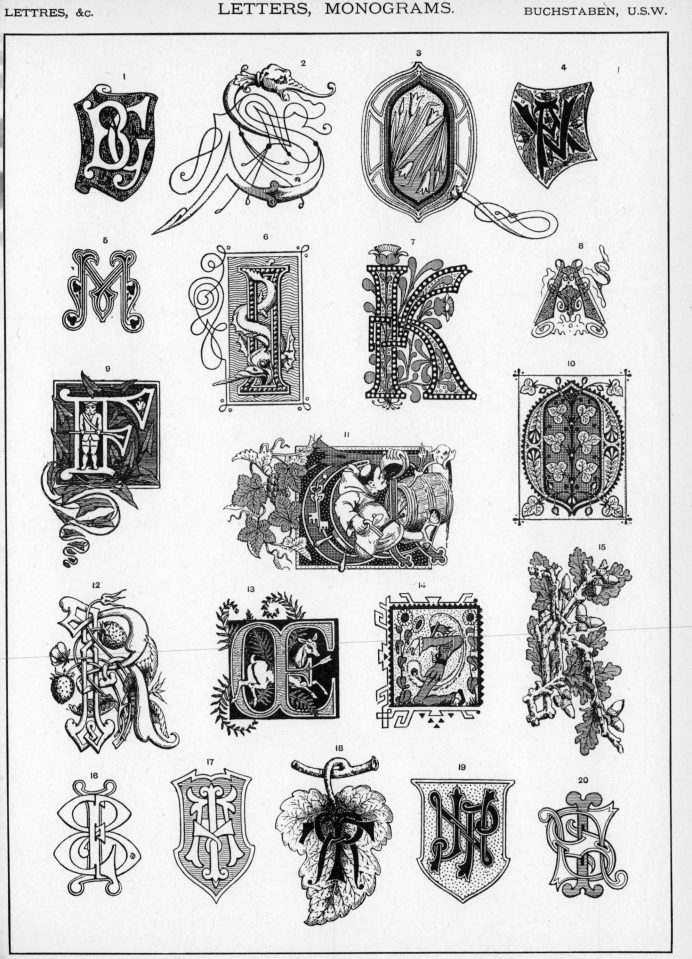

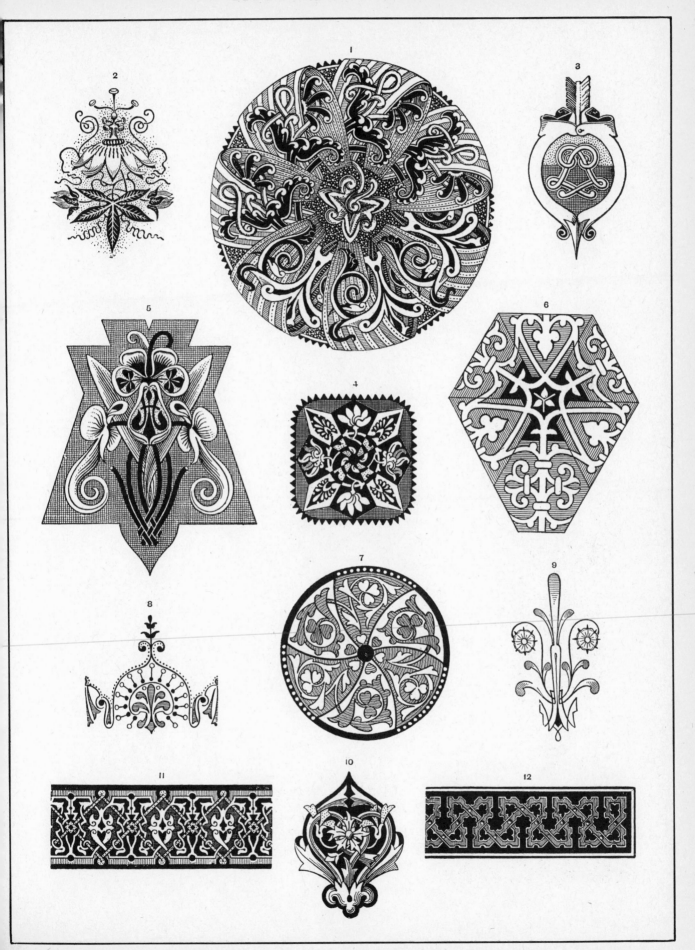

MISCELLANEOUS.

BY JOHN LEIGHTON, F.S.A.

Notes on the Plates

Savage and Early Tribes

Plate 1

1 and 2. What are called frets or meanders are common in all early work; of such are these rude frets, which are ancient Mexican.

3 is an ornament of somewhat similar character. Strange, uncouth variations of such forms, which possibly had a meaning of which we have no solution, are found in the ancient cities of Mexico and Central America. These ornaments are applicable to the enrichment of narrow bands of stonework or other material.

4 may have been suggested by feathers, and consists of gracefully flowing lines, fitting one into the other. They represent incised lines engraved on a plain surface.

5, 7, and 8 are enrichments for upright surfaces. The first appears like an impress in clay of a hieroglyphical character. 7 looks to be a series of birds' heads piled one upon another, as on a door post, and reminds one of the rude cats' heads of our own Norman work. 8 is evidently from matting. Similar zigzag lines are to be found worked out in many ways. The zig-zag has been noticed by various archæologists as being one of the earliest and most widely spread of all ornaments which are to be found among the most primitive works of mankind. We may easily imagine it commencing with the scratched lines on wet clay, or the alternate notching of a stick, as in Figs. 23 and 24.

Fig. 23 to Fig. 26

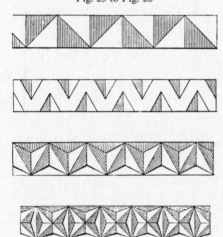

From this by an angular tool the workman soon arrived at the zig-zag formed by recessed triangles, Fig. 25, and the star-form, Fig. 26, all of which are common on the clubs of the South Sea Islanders. These ornaments are all monotonous, and simple repetitions of the same form. Repetition, however, is one of the means of giving pleasure to the eye, so common, that it is of constant occurrence in every known style or mode of ornamentation. It is equally frequent in nature.

6 is a peculiar example of a crowned figure, and may possibly represent a prisoner taken in battle, and condemned to occupy a confined and cramped position. The head has a beard, the biceps of the arm is indicated by a scroll, and although nearly bodiless, the knee, calf, and ankle-bone are clearly expressed, but in an odd conventional manner.

9 consists of flowing and interlacing lines, combined with faces, and running into a beak or species of bird's head at the top.

10 may represent a mask with large goggle eyes, mouth and tongue. It is after the manner of a tattoed face, as seen among the New Zealanders.

11 exhibits the use of colours, consisting of red, black, and white, and is apparently taken from leaning blocks, such as bricks, each being impressed with a stamp. If made continuous, it will be observed that the red and black alternate at regular intervals.

12 is a carved idol, which besides the rudely formed side figures of grotesque shapes, contains in the centre the suggestion of a face with two eyes, appearing as if rising above the triangle.

13 in ancient Mexican. It is strange and uncouth, without much beauty of form, and probably contains the name of some great personage or king, as the centre is formed of what appear to be arbitrary characters.

14 is a diaper with animal or cat's head, triangles and stripes. It also serves to show how prevalent geometrical figures were, even in the rudest ages. The angle squares contain a diagonal cross or saltire with square centre containing a diagonal square of the same breadth as the saltire. These angle squares might easily pass for mediæval tiles.

15, 16, and 17 are applicable for bands of stonework executed in relief or incised. 15 may have been suggested by steps added to an imperfect fret. 16 by the surf of the sea. A somewhat similar form is found in the Greek. 17 is an incised line consisting of two alternating semicircles dove-tailing into one another, looking like a folded ribbon or plaited cloth.

Many more rude yet highly suggestive forms might have been given, but these are considered sufficient, to give a tolerable idea of the primitive efforts of mankind in the ornamentation of surface.

Egyptian Ornamentation

Plate 2

1. Head crowned with leaves and buds. The beard and hair crimped horizontally as represented in Egyptian sculpture.

2. Frieze with flowers and buds in low relief growing from water.

3. Geometrical arrangement of leafage or palm grove, with crowned serpents below. The haje, or African cobra, when excited stands erect and swells out its body as here represented. The serpent was considered sacred in Egypt. It is not uncommon to find entire sculptured friezes and borders composed of a succession of these cobras, each surmounted by a disk to indicate their sacred character.

4. The papyrus in flower, bud, and seed. It is thus represented in low relief on the pedestal or altar in front of Hapimoon, the god of the Nile, with other aquatic offerings. The statue is in black granite, and is now in the British Museum. It was brought from Karnac.

5. Frieze or cavetto containing heads of the goddess Isis, which are thus found crowned with small temples (see also Fig. 34). The heads are alternated with serpents and palm-trees.

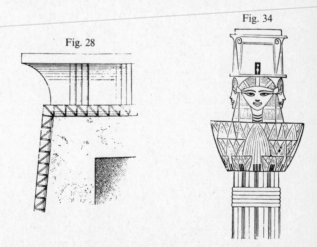

Fig. 28

Fig. 34

6. Leaf cornice. The only kind of cornice found (if it can be called a cornice) is formed by a large hollow springing from a torus or bold bead, as in Fig. 28.

7. Frieze of lotus and cartouche alternating. Hieroglyphics surrounded by an oval line either upright or horizontal, called a cartouche, are of frequent occurrence and indicate a proper name,

as that of a monarch, the one in the centre of this example reading KLEOPATRA. The two signs on either side of the lower bird indicate the feminine.

8. One half of a bell-shaped capital, developed or laid out flat. Many of the capitals have the upper portion or lip of the bell formed of four arcs of a circle surrounding a square, after the manner of a quatre-foil.

9. Lotus growing in water, with band of eyes and stars above. Water was usually represented by zigzag lines. The band containing the star indicated the heavens, and, probably, the eyes represented those of the deities, looking down upon the acts of men.

10. Symmetrical arrangement of elongated incised lines with lotus and buds.

11. Ornament formed of the lotus Band of reeds and vulture. The universal application of the lotus, or water-lily of the Nile, which was a sacred plant among the Egyptians, is very remarkable, and is found in every variety among the paintings and sculpture.

Plate 3

1. Baboons and fig-tree. The power of the Egyptian artists in expressing the character of animals by little more than simple outline was very remarkable.

2. Bundles of lotus with the haje or cobra surmounted by a globe or sun.

3. Spoon or ladle formed of a slave bearing on his head a bundle of reeds and lotus. In the Louvre and British Museum are many utensils ornamented by the lotus, but the use of the figure in this instance is somewhat questionable. There are examples also of a fish being converted into a dish, a hand into a scoop, &c., but such instances are rare. These conceits, however, are not confined to the Egyptians, for we find Etruscan and early Greek vases composed of figures and heads, with cavities in the cranium (Figs. 42, 43), or covered with rudely formed animals, Fig. 44, and Greek lamps made out of masks, feet, hands, animals, &c., but such applications are hardly within the province of refined taste.

4. Cobra with the disk and flower ornament.

5. Duck, showing the conventional treatment of the feathers as if formed of platted reeds.

6. Centre ornament formed of triple fish and lotus flower.

7 and 8. Painted bands, such as are found on mummy cases. See also Fig. 41.

9. Star-form tile or diaper.

10. The winged globe, accompanied by asps, the type of the sun, a sacred emblem of the highest order, and usually placed over the entrances to the temples. The wings are supposed to be those of the hawk, and are also symbolical of the sun, on account of the elevation to which this bird continued its flight, and of the faculty which it was considered to have, of looking at the sun with a steady gaze.

11. Bold lotus treatment with flowers, being the same in all four ways that it is looked at. The flat ceilings of the temples were usually covered by painting in this manner.

12. Frieze formed of bearded heads ornamented with head-dresses of banded reeds, alternating with lotus buds.

Plate 4

1. Lotus and aquatic plants bound together and arranged symmetrically.

2. Fan-shaped standard ornament.

3. Lotus band. Many of the mummy coverings, as in the British Museum, have bands and enrichments of this character, executed in gold and colour. See Fig. 41, also incised as Fig. 45.

4. Emblem of security alternating with buds.

5 and 6. Diapers or tiles.

7. Throne bound by aquatic plants and the lotus of the Nile, emblematical of Egypt and its fertility.

8. Lotus flowers and buds growing on the water.

9. Border formed of a row of temples on a river. An example of doubtful taste, and rather to be avoided.

10. Band for painting. Bound reeds with lotus flowers and buds.

11. Bundle of lotus with the emblem of security and feather crest.

12. Papyrus with emblems of stability above.

13. Ornamental frieze or band divided by reeds with cartouches and hieroglyphic writing.

14 and 15. Papyrus and lotus. Fig. 45 represents the lotus as incised in granite, from the collar of a figure upon the cover of a sarcophagus in the British Museum.

16. Decorated cartouche or shield.

17. Circular ornament with lotus growing in water.

Fig. 41

Fig. 42

Fig. 43

Fig. 44

Fig. 45

Fig. 46

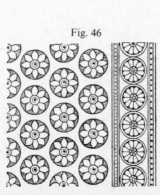

Fig. 47

Fig. 48

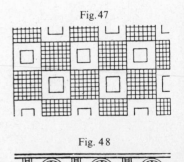

Assyrian Ornamentation

Plate 5

1. Lotus and bud ornament, evidently a reminiscence of some of the Egyptian ornamentation, enamelled or inlaid with colour.
2. Lotus and bud ornamentation sculptured in low relief, after the manner of that forming a border to the pavement from the palace at Nimroud, now in the British Museum.
3 to 9. Small ornaments, parts of thrones and chairs from the wall sculptures.
10. Centre ornament, giving four different varieties or terminations after the manner of those found among the Assyrian sculptures.
11. Foot of sculptured chair or throne.
12. Castellated termination, suggested by forms found among the sculptures.
13. Palm flower from the terminals of the sacred tree, probably the origin of the Greek honeysuckle.
14 and 15. Centre ornaments.
16. Wave and bandolette pattern for painting.
17. Fan and fir-cone ornament. The fir-cone frequently occurs in Assyrian ornament, and some of the priests in the sculptures have fir-cones in their hands.
18. Fir-cone and lotus-bud ornament, somewhat resembling the patterns found edging the robes of the Assyrian kings. The fir-cone is symbolical of fire, the lotus of water.
19. Fan or Palm ornament and alternating bud with guilloche band below. These are found executed in black and white in a species of glazed earthenware tile.
20. Reeded columns with lotus-bud capitals supporting reel and bead, from Persepolis.
21. Opening bud and fir-cone border, from the edgings to the draperies of the figures in the sculptures.

Plate 6

1. Eagle-headed lions and ornament, designed in the Assyrian manner.
2. Rosette or patera. These are of frequent occurrence in the sculptures, as in the pavement from the palace at Nimroud, forming bands of ornament which divide the whole into squares, the squares being filled in with fir-cones and the expanded lotus.
3. Fan or palm ornament in metal filled in with enamel in two colours, from Nineveh. A form of flower which is probably the origin of the Greek honeysuckle.
4 and 5. Enrichments from the bases of columns found at Persepolis. These are not strictly Assyrian, but in a closely allied style.
6. Colossal eagle-headed and winged lion, after the remains found at Nineveh and Persepolis. These monsters, found guarding the portals of Assyrian palaces, may in many respects be taken as models of appropriate conventional treatment of animal forms, the majestic strength of the creature being well maintained without a too literal imitation of nature, the graceful attributes of the bird being combined with that of the quadruped. The winged bulls and human-headed lions in the British Museum have the forelegs straighter than in our example, and consequently they have a greater appearance of strength. They have also, when viewed diagonally, five legs. This is a defect which is caused by the attempting to combine semi with whole relief. The muscles of the legs are very much exaggerated.
7. Sacred tree and pomegranates. These sacred trees occur upon the sculptures in different forms, often with priests or winged eagle-headed figures on either side, with a fir-cone in one hand advanced towards the tree, and a vessel in the form of a bucket in the other, said to be symbolical of the sacred elements, fire and water.
8. Sacred ornament with acorn terminations.
9. Diaper and fringe from the sculptured hangings upon the chariot horses. Many of the dresses, harness, and other accessories upon the king's robes, their chariots and horses, are elaborately ornamented and executed with minute delicacy. See Figs. 46, 47, and 48, already given.
10. Bas-relief diaper from the sculptures, inclosed pateras and semi-pateras. The sculptures which lined the walls of the palaces were invariably in very low relief, never casting deep shadows or violating that appearance of solidity and flatness so desirable in mural decoration.
11. Twin lions, after the manner of an Assyrian sword-hilt. The capitals of columns from Persepolis are frequently formed with double heads in this manner. Double-headed capitals are also found in the Indian, as may be seen in the sculpture of the cast of the gateway from the Sanchi Tope in the South Kensington Museum.
12. Enrichment from the capital of a column from Persepolis.
13. Sculptured base from a Persepolitan column.

Greek Ornamentation

Plate 7

1. A free adaptation of the anthemion ornament. Many varieties of it are found on Greek vases.
2. The honeysuckle and lotus alternating, but not connected by scroll work, as in the anthemion ornament. The arrangement is after the manner of the Egyptian, from which the Greek ornament was derived.
3 are examples of flower-form ornaments, usually termed pateræ, frequently found in Greek architecture. Derived from the Assyrian.
4. A simple form of frieze ornament for painting.
5 and 6. Atlantes, given as suggestions for introducing in front of a pier or pilaster to support the entablature above. See also 4, Plate 10.

The idea of these male figures, which are sometimes called Telamones or giants, is taken from the temple of Agrigentum, where they are represented supporting the superincumbent weight upon their head and arms.
7. A four-way wave scroll, forming a panel for inlay or painted decoration.
8, 9, 10, 11, 12 contain suggestions for meander or fret form for gold and colour, alternating with square enrichments containing animal, vegetable, and fish forms. Frets are of constant occurrence in Greek painting. Other variations will be found in Plates 8, 9, 11, and 12.

Plate 8

1. Frieze enrichment, somewhat after the manner of those from the Erechtheum. See Figs. 61 and 62.
2. Anthemion ornament reversed and alternated.
3 to 10. Various suggestions for narrow band enrichments, in character similar to those found on Greek vases.
11. Trident forms of enrichment for coloured decoration.
12. Heart-form enrichment; arranged in a circle for colour on a gold ground.
13. Honeysuckle and scroll enrichment issuing from an acanthus leaf.
14. Circle containing chimera treading upon a snake, with a border formed of the wave ornament.

Fig. 61

Fig. 62

Plate 9

1. Disk containing the heads of the Fates.
2 and 3. Heads of Minerva with borders of bud forms.
4 and 5. Continuous ivy enrichments, as found on Greek vases.
6. Altar with Pan and Bacchante.
7 and 8. Circles containing a vase with foliage, also ivy, vine, grapes, and laurel, similar to examples found on vases.
9. Fret band.
10 and 11. Diagonal foliated enrichments for borders.
12. The honeysuckle and lotus, with flowers and scroll work, but having an Assyrian or archaic Greek character.

Plate 10

1. Honeysuckle and lotus with pateræ.
2 and 3. Enrichments after the manner of the antefixal ornaments which formed the finish of the roof tiles on temples.
4. Telamon supporting a frieze enriched by the echinus or egg-and-tongue ornament.
5 and 6. Wave-line honeysuckle and ivy ornaments, after the manner of those found on Greek vases.
7. Double or reversed lotus ornament.
8. A variation upon the anthemion ornament.
9, 10, and 11. Leaf ornaments, for painting in the style of the Greek vases.

Plate 11

1. Centre leaf ornament, the two sides varied.
2 and 3. Ivy-leaf ornaments.
4. Leaf border with tendrils.
5. Honeysuckle and scroll: panel-painting, blue on gold ground.
6. Marble inlay for pavement or wall decoration.
7. Meander fret border, with angle ornament for a ceiling, in colour or low relief.
8, 9, 10, and 11. Continuous leaf ornaments for narrow bands or borders.
12, 13, 14, 15, 17, and 18. Border enrichments of various design, for painting or inlay.
16. One portion of continuous leaf or flower enrichment.

Plate 12

1. Brush-formed ornament, with inclosing lines.
2. Honeysuckle centre, with flowering scrolls and leafage for painting.
3. Centre enrichment, with line interlaced scrolls and honeysuckles.
4. Painted panel. Goddess on a winged wheel, with meander border.
5. Heart-form scroll and honeysuckle border.
6. Frieze or border, with enriched panels and fretwork.
7. Hanging honeysuckle ornament.
8. Honeysuckle within heart-form, with branching scrolls and leafage, after the manner of foliage frequently found on the Greek vases.

Greek & Etruscan Ornamentation

Plate 13

1 and 2. Heads and foliage, after the manner of a more free and careless brush form, evidently done with great rapidity, such as is sometimes found on the later vases. Some of the scrolls were painted in white.
3. Mirror frame with a foliated border in engraved metal work. In the centre a flower for jewelry, with horned head and pendants varied.
4. Border enrichment form, with egg-and-fan or honeysuckle, for sculpture in low relief.
5. Convolvulus ornament, with leafage of a more natural type, for engraved metal work.
6. Border ornament, consisting of lotus and honeysuckle transposed alternately.
7. Cup-and-fan ornament or lily interlaced, for a band or frieze.
8. Suggestion for sculpture. Cupid stringing his bow.

9 and 10. Fan and bud ornaments for bronze work in low relief.
11. Cock for flat painting on crackled gold ground, and border with scroll and honeysuckles. The corner ornaments varied.

Pompeian Ornamentation

Plate 14

1. Painted arabesque for narrow panel.
2. Grotesque panel painted in relief. All kinds of animals, monsters, and children were thus introduced in the most incongruous manner.
3. Wall decoration, painted in the brightest hues, with arabesque borders varied, the centre in perspective as if seen through an opening.
4. Arabesque pilaster or filling for panel.
5 and 7. Painted borders.
6. Dolphin brought in with scroll-work. Griffins and many other animals were often most playfully intermingled with the foliage.

Roman Ornamentation

Plate 15

1 and 2. Animals, monsters, and various chimeræ were commonly introduced by the Romans among their carvings, such as sea-horses, 1; or griffins with their extremities running off into scroll foliage, as in 2.
3 and 4. What are called *termini* are characteristic features in Roman decoration and furniture. The *terminus* or terminal was a form commencing with a head, and sometimes shoulders, finishing with feet, with claws, or with a plinth at bottom, the intermediate space being filled with a square portion tapering downwards. 3 is a terminal emblematical of Bacchus, filled in with the thyrsus and grape vine; 4, indicative of the god Mercury upon the globe, with cap and wings attached to the head and wings to the feet, the centre being filled with the caduceus or wand of Mercury.
5 and 6. Comic and tragic masks. The Greeks and Romans usually wore masks in their theatrical performances, hence masks are often found used as ornaments.
7. We have not many examples of Roman wall paintings; but there can be little doubt that their rooms were decorated by painting of the most elegant description. 7 represents an ornamental fountain of fanciful design, such as may have been used for a panel in wall decoration, or might be suitable for carving in low relief.
8 and 9 are ornaments arranged after the manner of masks.

Plate 16

1 and 2. Female head flanked with monsters. 1, lion winged with bird's claws; 2, bird with animal's hind legs. For carving in low relief.
3 and 4. Rings in bronze for gates. The one represents the head of a satyr, the other a conventional lion's head.
5 and 6. Running ornaments for painting.
5, a variation of the egg-and-tongue; and 6 after the type of the Greek anthemion ornament.
7. A double-bodied sphinx supporting a pedestal carrying a lamp, flanked by sitting female figures representing Industry and Law, with a back-ground formed by the rays of the rising sun. Applicable to wall decoration in painting or low relief.
8 and 9. Painted or inlay ornaments for pilasters or upright panels.
10 and 11. Terminal angles of altars. 10, winged lion and foot, with shaft of column with twisted flute and foliated base. 11, griffin's head terminating in a horse's hoof.
12. Female terminal figure in the centre, from the base of which springs foliated scroll-work, carrying flower-baskets. For painted decoration.

Plate 17

1, 4, 5, 6, 7, 9, and 10 are ornaments more after the Etruscan manner, but such as may reasonably be supposed to have been used in their painted decoration by the Romans, who frequently employed

Etruscan artists in their house decoration.

1. Foliated ornament for cresting or border.
2. Ornament formed upon the honeysuckle, and with acanthus foliage.
3. Ornamental fluting for columns or for carving in wood-work for a dado or other purpose.
4, 5, 6, and 7. Upright running ornaments for painting, containing branching foliage and flowers; leaf and berries, upon a wave line; a variation upon the Vitruvian scroll, with the reel and bead; and ivy with berries.
8. Fanciful mask of Neptune with beard worked into dolphins and trident: eyebrows and hair formed of sea-weed and earrings of escallop shells.
9, 10, 11, and 12. Ornaments or borders for inlay or painting.
13. Surface decoration in relief.
14. Bracket formed with African elephant's head at the angle; the centre flower and festoons interlacing with the animal's trunk.
15. Tablet with pendant, buffalo or ox's skull with swag of fruit and flowers. The ox's skull was frequently used in Roman ornament and decoration. See Fig. 101.

Fig. 101

Plate 18

1, 2, and 3. Medallions. 1, head with dolphin helmet; 2, the triumph of Love; 3, Romulus and Remus suckled by the wolf, emblematical of the foundation of Rome.
4. Terminal composition for a base, suitable for sculpture.
5 and 6. Acorn and grape batons.
7. Ornament in the form of a horn, with foliations springing from a boar's head.
8. Central composition of swans and foliage, suitable for carving.
9. Bracket supporting statuette of a Bacchante flanked with scrolls.
10 and 11. Grotesque centre. Comic mask with side scrolls, supporting (10) conventional eagle with foliated wings, and (11) conventional winged panther.

Plate 19

1 and 2. Roman altar or pedestal with shield of Minerva in the centre, containing the head of Medusa, the Gorgon, supported by a cupid. The left side finished with a fluted pilaster and foliated frieze panel, with a terminal figure in profile; the right-hand side pilaster panelled and filled in with interlacing vine foliage with grapes and birds. Ram's head terminal in profile.
3 and 4. Grotesque lion and ram's heads, for application to ornamental purposes.
5. Cupid with foliated termination carrying a basket.
6. Panel in relief: the head of the Gorgon Medusa, and claws of harpy.
7. Trophy with heads of Hercules, Ajax, and Agamemnon, accompanied by lion's skin and clubs arranged ornamentally.
8. Angle terminal.
9. Centre terminal. Convolvulus, horse-shoe and hoofs.
10. Dolphin terminal or angle of pedestal.
11. Angle of pedestal flanked by cornucopia, the ever-fruitful horn of Amalthea. The angle filled with reaping-hook and corn.
12. Border formed of spiral line and convolvulus bell.

Plate 20

1. Ornamental composition in bas-relief, containing boy in vase with two cupids, scroll-work, and ram's head.
2 and 3. Ornamental vase with varied sides for carving.
4. Frieze in bas-relief, with boys as warriors, cupids, birds, animals, and reptiles, among the foliage.
5. Fret inlay for wood panelling or marquetry.

6. Scroll-work border of foliage with swans, fountain, and fish, for painted decoration.
7. Fret border for painting or inlay.
8 and 9. Fretwork for inlay or mosaic. Similar examples are found in ancient pavements shaded as in 9.[1]

Chinese Ornamentation

Plate 21

In the panel 1 the picturesque treatment of the bamboo, with the hanging vase, the gracefully arranged flowers and foliage, and the life added to the composition by the birds and insects, is very pleasing, and in the Chinese manner, although it may not be very high art. If looked at as a "motif" for panel decoration, it offers an excellent suggestion, and should be worked out in colours on a light toned or a gold ground.
2 is three fans arranged triangularly in a circle, with intermediate flowers on a gold ground.
3 consists of three overlying circles, in a trefoil form upon a fish-scale ground, containing geometrically formed four-petalled flowers.
4 is formed by a diagonal zigzag line in two colours with filling-in of flowers and leaves, applicable to textile stuffs.
5. A panel showing the conventional treatment of a female figure in a garden. The borders are made up with flowers and other forms peculiar to the Chinese.
6 has a fret-formed square panel in a circle containing a flower. Around the circle is a border with trefoil foliage flowing from the circle, the oblong sides being filled up with geometrical forms and flowers.
7 contains dragons or hydras, with corner flowers and "crackle" filling-up in the spandrels. These grotesque and quaintly drawn dragons frequently occur, and form highly characteristic features in Chinese ornamentation. They typify the evil spirit which is supposed to exist in the world, and when placed on roofs are sometimes shown as pinned down to the building by a sword. The idea is the same as the superstition in this country of the horse-shoe nailed over the door, to prevent the entrance of all warlocks and witches. The Chinese notion of an eclipse is represented by a golden ball, with a monster of the dragon species floating in mid air, and supposed to be advancing with open jaws to swallow up the golden orb which indicates the sun. Thus they typify what they consider to be evils, as dreadfully ugly monsters, ready to appear out of darkness to engulf them in their enormous jaws.
8 is from a heart-shaped hand screen or fan, containing a dragon vase from which grows a rose, supported on a flower-stand with earth and side foliage.
9 has a flower represented symmetrically on each side of the centre of a hand screen or fan, issuing from a shell. The flowers are in colours upon a gold "crackle" ground. This crackle is taken from the china, in which the glaze has been cracked by heat or time, and therefore such examples are supposed to be of ancient date. In modern work the crackle is frequently imitated by painted lines, and its origin is found in the Chinaman's love of the antique, and his desire to reproduce the effects of time or imperfectly glazed specimens of early workmanship.

Japanese Ornamentation

Plate 22

1. Aquatic birds and river plants, all full of expression. Japanese treatment of circular figures is very various.
2. An unsymmetrical arrangement of interlaced lilies.
3. A wheel or spring form, as if in movement.
4. A curious diaper of conventional birds swimming on water, represented as looking down upon them.

---

[1] All decorations of pavements should be by flat ornament and not shaded as if in relief. If applied to a wall surface the decoration may with propriety be executed in relief, but not shaded if in flat ornament.

5. Birds as seen in rain.
6. Sections of flowers unsymmetrically arranged.
7. Bird pattern arranged symmetrically.
8. Birds and flower brought into a circle.
9. Butterfly diaper; the insects being placed bi-symmetrically and counterchanged in colours.
10. Square on octagonal form, placed on the key or fret diaper, similar to what is found in the Chinese, Fig. 112.
11. Conventional flower decoration.
12. Natural flowers on a conventional form.

Plate 23

1 presents an interesting example of the symmetrical arrangements which are occasionally met with. It embraces a great variety of objects, very cleverly disposed and full of life, as if on the sea-shore: a crab in the centre, with lobsters on each side, dolphins and flying-fish; one of the flying-fish forming the centre over the crab being represented skimming the distant water and approaching towards us. The breakers on the shore are very conventionally rendered, giving the whole an odd mixture and quaint conceit, which is far from being unpleasing.

2. Classic forms imitative of Greek or Roman furniture are sometimes met with in Japanese works, as in this example, which represents a tripod-chair in which is placed a vase of flowers. It is probably a recollection from books shown them by missionaries or others from the West. An imitative people are sure to be struck with any new form they may see.

3 contains some of their peculiar fret-forms growing from a bulb, the whole being arranged in the form of a trefoil issuing from a circle.

4 is a conventional and yet lifelike arrangement of interlaced fish surrounded by a narrow border of water, which partakes of the general outline, and by its dark colour throws up the fish with great distinctness.

5 is somewhat of the same character as 3, taking up the vase-form, which is filled in with fret and leaf ornaments.

6 is a landscape, with bird of prey evidently intent upon the fish, which is attempting to ascend the cascade. The sun with clouds, the gnarled trunk of the tree, and the plants in the foreground are all worth noticing, and are highly characteristic of Japanese art when representing nature.

7 shows two overlapping circles, as may have been suggested by seals or coins. The first contains a fan, with a floor indicated by fret-work, and the sky studded with stars. The underlying circle has a wheel form of eight arms indicated in two colours. Pattern upon pattern, and form upon form, is by no means uncommon in Eastern art, but the way in which circular patches are placed upon frets and grounds is peculiar to China and Japan.

Plate 24

1. Four-petalled flowers contained in continuous vesicas, the colours alternately change on each side the centre line. The lower margin contains a ribbon border.

2. Hexagonal figure formed with bamboo, the articulations of the stem forming the angles, from three of which issue a triple arrangement of leaves, the centre ones meeting in the centre of the circle and the lateral ones turning down to the unoccupied angles. The ground is spread with flowers irregularly.

3 is a hexagon with three spirally-formed petals, alternating with what are apparently meant for stamens.

4. Fans, a damio's device. An odd admixture of animal and vegetable life, among which is seen a portion of a sculptured head in bas-relief. The birds among the reeds, the animal climbing a tree, the mermaid and her offspring, and the triple arrangement of the leaves of the water-lily, each of which also contains the flower,—but, above all, the poor old horse standing shivering in the wind up to his fetlocks in rank coarse grass, which is evidently not inviting to his palate,—all show what intensity of expression these artists are able to throw into comparatively minor objects. Not a line out of place or that could be spared.

5 is a fret diaper in two colours, carried diagonally by a Z-like line.

6 is a leaf border with fret edge on a matted ground.

7 is a treble diagonal key-fret border, with zigzag edges and circles in the intervals.

8 contains one of these extraordinary conventional birds, which, although so unlike anything in nature, is yet full of life and vigour. The clouds are indicated by curiously formed curly outlines.

9 is a border formed of the nautilus, sailing on a conventional sea, with the sand of the sea-shore in the foreground, and curiously formed clouds above.

10 has a triple leaf-formed arrangement, with a spur or three-pronged figure in the centre.

11. An S-form on oval flower.

12 represents a tortoise and aquatic animals among reeds and bamboo.

13. Fish with water and land back-ground. Nothing seems to come amiss to the Japanese,—every form in nature is introduced in some shape or other. Whatever does not in any way accord with their ideas of the beautiful is altered by them at once, and rendered in their own odd, conventional manner.

Indian Ornamentation

Plate 25

1. Upright outline ornamentation of conventional forms, which have occasionally a slight resemblance to the classic. Often again filled in with minute detail.
2. Conventional growing ornament.
3. Vase and flowers, arranged after the manner of a branching tree.
4 and 5. Foliated sprigs.
6. Superficial pattern, for woven fabric in colours.
7. Pear and heart shaped ornament, with flowers slightly varied from nature.
8. Pine-cone section, for shawl or other woven fabric.
9. Symmetrical and non-symmetrical ornament combined in symmetrical outline, for colour.
10. Symmetrical growing pattern, for raised work or for two colours.
11. Symmetrical disjointed pattern, for raised work, inlay or colour.
12. Flowing feather-formed flower border, for colour.
13. Border of alternating and flowing triple leaf in red and gold.

Plate 26

1. Cross arrangement of heart-formed leaves, diapered with foliage.
2. Upright branch-leaved ornament.
3. Foliated heart-form symmetrical ornament.
4. Surface decoration growing from central octafoil filled in with cross form and foliage. The star completed by eight lobes of leaf form.
5 and 6. Sprigs conventionalized from nature.
7 and 8. Upright patterns of symmetrical ornament for coloured decoration or inlay.
9 and 10. Flowing and upright borders, for lace or other delicate work.
11. Border to use any way. Red ornament with gold bead or pearled outline upon black.
12. Disjointed diamond border in blue, white, and gold.
13. Flowing wave-line flower and leaf border for carving in low relief or inlay in hard wood, the lines engraved and filled in black.
14. Diagonal bordering filled in with double pine and branched leaves. The following diagonal form to be reversed so as to leave a triangle between filled in with half leaf-form flower.
15 and 16. Sprig-form flowers on ornamental forms. Indian detail fits one part into another so that the whole surface is covered with minute form or intricate combinations of colour.

Fig. 112

Persian Ornamentation

Plate 27

1. Pine-cone flaming ornament. Fire worship has been a widespread superstition among the Persians, hence the prevalence of flowing flame form.

2 and 3. Conventional scroll engraved borders for metal work, filled in with black varnish.

4. Peacock on inverted vase. The spreading tail is developed by eyes, which would be enriched by the most brilliant colours, the breast of the bird being contrasted by dark blue sheen of greenish hue.

5 and 6. Borders of conventional ornament, which have a strong affinity to the Moresque. These would be enriched by various colours, or engraved on metal.

7 and 8. Small upright engraved ornaments.

9, 10, and 11. Central ornaments for glazed tiles or other works, with natural leaves of the ivy, &c.

12. Ornament for shawl or other textile fabric; the colours being harmoniously blended and intermingled as indicated by lines.

13 and 14. Fanciful forms filled with characteristic ornament, allied to the Indian, which it frequently closely resembles.

Moorish or Saracenic Ornamentation

Plate 28

1. Interlaced ornament with foliage.

2 and 3. Upright borders—interlaced fret, and foliage with interlaced form.

4. Symmetrical flowing form. It is a common characteristic feature in Moorish ornament for one form to be flowing round and fitting in to fill up the interstices left by another form.

5 and 6. Small symmetrical ornaments.

7 and 8. Outline centres of foliated and interlacing form.

9 and 10. Flowing, angular, and interlaced terminals.

11. Geometrical diaper.

12. Interlaced square and diagonal design, with cross-form foliage in the centre.

13. Interlaced geometrical design for tile flooring or parquetry.

14. Interlaced outline ornament.

Plate 29

1. Arabesque pierced stone battlement inlaid with flat foliage.

2 and 3. Upright ornaments, honeysuckle and pine.

4. Geometrical and foliated centre ornament. Form laid upon form.

5. Cross-form pine ornament.

6. Eight-pointed star filled with radiating foliage, in oval or vesica; the intermediate space being diapered with pointed ogee line from star, and foliage.

7 and 8. Oblong centres for panel decoration in colour.

9. Interlaced fret tile pattern. There is a great variety of patterns, somewhat similar to this, to be found in the wall decoration of the Alhambra, all formed by the intersection of equidistant lines, and which, Owen Jones observes, could be traced through the Arabian to the Greek fret. A peculiarity, however, which the Moorish fret possesses is the addition of the diagonal line, without which the power of interlacing would be greatly limited.

10. Flowing foliated upright form for colour or engraving.

11. Panel in low relief for colour with shield surrounded by foliage. The Moors occasionally introduced the shield charged with armorial bearings, but not very frequently. The elaborate diapers and other designs on the walls, and other parts, in the Alhambra are all worked in low relief in plaster and afterwards picked out in colour and gold.

Plate 30

1. Upright flower interlaced with geometrical trilobed line.

2 and 3. Conventional foliated forms with semi-conventional leafage.

4. Pointed quatrefoil centre filled in with foliage.

5 and 6. Damascene ornaments for metal.

7. Geometrical superficial ornament for colour or inlay.

8 and 9. Geometrical outlines for diapers, which may be further filled in with foliage according to the scale of the work or the degree of richness required.

10. Arabian scrolls working one into the other, as is so frequently the practice in the style.

11. Disjointed interlacing ornament.

12 and 13. Oblong panel decoration formed with flowing and interlaced line and heart-form centre filled in with foliage. The two sides varied.

Plate 31

1 and 2. Oblong panel formed with interlaced fret-form square centre, carried into scroll foliage. Two sides varied.

3 and 4. Terminal flowers. Conventionalized harts'-tongue leaf and honeysuckle.

5. Centre ornament for panel in low relief, and colour, interlacing foliated forms.

6 and 7. Geometrical upright diapers for paper or wall decoration.

8 and 9. Interlacing arabesque foliage, for colour and slight relief.

10. Double triangle in circle, interlacing with hexagonal form and circles.

11 and 12. Interlaced square and diagonal lines, with foliage for diaper or panel decoration.

These designs do not follow literally the principles found in Arabesque ornament, but are intended to suggest the application of a few of their ingenious and beautiful lines to the purposes of modern ornamentation.

Byzantine Ornamentation

Plate 32

1. Interlaced cross-form in square, for execution in low flat relief. Byzantine.

2. Celtic initial letter I, after the manner of the Anglo-Saxon manuscripts, with skeleton animal.

3. Interlacing pearl-work, with nail-head border. Norman or Celtic.

4. Double bird and scroll work, somewhat after the manner of the Anglo-Saxon manuscripts. To be worked in gold and colour.

5 and 6. Circles containing cockatrice and stag, eccentrically twisted.

7. Band of interlaced ribbon and foliage.

8 and 9. Interlaced geometrical combinations for inlay.

Plate 33

1. Dragons in low relief for the tympanum of a doorway of Anglo-Norman character, interlaced in the Celtic manner. The two sides are varied.

2. Diaper in low relief and picked out in colour, finishing with cresting upon top.

3. Emblematical form of fish, eagle, and serpent united—a symbol of Christian evangelism.

4. Cherubim with heads formed of the emblems of the four evangelists. Wings covered with eyes to symbolize the all-seeing presence of the Deity.

5. Upright ornament with interlaced animal form.

6. String-course of bird monsters forming scrolls. Anglo-Norman or Celtic.

7. Frieze of sharp-lobed Byzantine foliage, arranged in the manner of the Greek anthemion ornament. Many varieties of the anthemion ornament are to be found in Byzantine ornamentation. A heart-form arrangement, evidently upon the same type, is of frequent occurrence. See Fig. 178.

Fig. 178

8. Interlaced star-formed frieze. These star patterns are sometimes found in the Byzantine, but are more frequent in Moorish work, in which they are sometimes carried out in the most intricate manner. The animals' heads indicate that the work is Byzantine, as animal form is never introduced in the Moorish.

Plate 34

1. Norman bas-relief, having the Celtic character of interlacing long-necked animal form with foliage.
2 and 3. Foliated animal form in the Celtic manner, as found in Anglo-Saxon manuscripts.
4. Alternating fret-formed diaper for colour or low relief. Forms of a similar character are found sculptured in low relief on the Irish crosses.
5 and 6. Borders or string-courses, in upright formed design of Byzantine or Romanesque character.
7. Double dragon scroll of Celtic or Irish character.
8 and 9. Drop and final ornaments.
10. Byzantine foliated enrichment for execution in low relief.
11. Cross heart-form panel for painting.
12. Panel for painting or inlay. Diamond and semicircles interlaced.

Gothic Ornamentation

Plate 35

1 represents a seal after the mediæval manner. A figure under a canopy, seated on a throne representing vigilance (the greyhound) and power (the lion), between two angels, who are presenting the one a book, and the other a shield.
2. Vesica panel with St. Michael supported by saints overcoming the evil one. The lion of St. Mark below.
3, 4, 5, 6, 7. Tracery panels of various design for metal-work. Small tracery work of this character was much in use for locks and plates during the fifteenth century. Many specimens are very elaborately cut. The metal was usually in plates of several thicknesses fastened together with pins or bolts. The ground was sometimes covered with scarlet cloth, or decorated by painting, as is 7.
8. One compartment of an oak rood-screen (style fifteenth century). The figure introduced in the open-work above is an outline for painting.
9. A band or freize of flowing tracery, of late fourteenth-century character.
10. A square boss for carving in oak. Fifteenth-century character.

Plate 36

1. Vesica under a canopy with the pascal lamb, and monogram "John Lambe;" for engraving on brass or other metal.
2. Decorated or fourteenth-century flowing tracery, from the back of the altar, Beverley Minster.
3. Angle of panel with carved frame consisting of tracery and foliage, with painted and gilded panel in the centre.
4. Panel for wood-work, with vine-leaves and grapes.
5. Vesica with angel carrying a shield emblazoned with the sun of Christianity enlightening the Negro, emblematical of the motto, "Lord, lighten our darkness." Composition for painting.
6. Panel for wood-carving (fifteenth century) with head of king

Fig. 206   Fig. 207

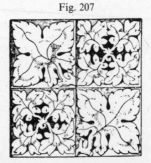

with sceptre. Crowned heraldic shield with monogram and supporters. Linen-fold panel below.
7. Ornamental fillet.
8. Late French Flamboyant Gothic tracery panelling, for pierced carved work in hardwood or ivory.
9. Tracery panel for carving, with paintings or inlay of boar and fawn.
10 to 16. Compartments for stone carved diapers, each division by repetition forming a separate and distinct pattern. Examples of stone diaper work are to be found in Westminster Abbey, Beverley Minster, Winchelsea Church, &c.—See also Figs. 206, 207.

Plate 37

Design for a book cover, the New Testament, and back for the same, in naturalesque Gothic. Among the foliage is introduced the lily as the emblem of purity, and the passion-flower as emblematical of the passion of our Lord. In the centre is the cross with the sacred monogram. The dove as emblematic of the Holy Spirit descending from above within a triangle for the Trinity and a circle for eternity. The cross as emblematical of Christianity vanquishes the evil spirit, which is represented as a winged serpent in the act of falling. In the corners are the emblems of the evangelists, and the capitals of the slender columns are formed by angels bearing shields containing the emblems of the passion. The back contains a vesica, in which is the Holy Virgin and Child, surmounted by the heart and cross, with angels at the sides in adoration. The foliage is composed of the rose, ivy, and lily.

Plate 38

1. Late German-Gothic panel with bordered vesica containing painting or low-relief carving of the Virgin and Child, with the emblems of the evangelists at the corners.
2. Panel with flowing tracery, containing shield with heraldic double-headed eagle, for carving or metal work.
3. Carved oak panel, French Flamboyant tracery. The Flamboyant form of tracery is also found occasionally in English work, as in the west front of York Cathedral, and other buildings. The English artists, however, did not carry it to excess as in France. Although it was adopted in late Decorated work, the flowing forms were soon neglected for the Perpendicular, which form of tracery was never adopted by French artists. Hence the reason for their carrying the Flamboyant to such an excess.
4. Head of tracery panelling having interlaced lily foliage, with heart-form filled with branched radiating triple foliage.
5. Lily in interlaced tracery form, with flat strawberry foliage, flowers and fruit, and thistle leaves.
6, 7. Tracery panels with foliage, for carving or metal work.
8. A suggestion for the combination of foliage and tracery, with crowned pine and heart. The parts blacked in are pierced. Suitable for embossing.

Plate 39

1. Vesica panel filled with geometrical and flowing Decorated tracery.
2, 9, 11, 12, 13, 14. Forms of plate tracery for metal work.
4. Canopied head of niche, for metal work.
5. Head of angle niche, for carving in oak.
3, 6, 7, 10. Small oblong and circular tracery panels for carving. Might be applied to furniture.
8. Flowing tri-form panel, representing the burial of the dead, the passage of the river Lethe after death, and the ascension into heaven.

Plate 40 (Superficial)

1. Decorative panel; conventional arrangement of the rose.
2 and 3. Decorative and geometrical forms for wall-papers or draperies.
4. Upright design for heraldic crowned shield and supporters, with circular and flowing lines combined.
5 to 22. Designs for encaustic tiles or squares for repetition as diapers for painted wall decoration,—comprising, among other forms, interlacing lines, rose and crown, lily, fleur-de-lis, rose,

shamrock, and thistle, maple leaf, horse-chestnut leaf, dolphin, crosses, and lion.
23. Royal arms with Tudor rose, oak and acorns (England).
24. Diaper containing a combination of the thistle, St. Andrew's cross, and fleur-de-lis (Scotland).
25. Combination of flowing lines with harp, shamrock, and stars (Ireland).—The last three designs are intended for painted wall decoration, or might be adapted to bookbinding or other flat surface.

Ornamental Metal Work

Plate 41

1. Portion of cast-iron grille or railing with wrought-iron twisted spike.
2. Wrought-iron cross in plate-metal; lower portion in cast work, with angels, heart, and crown.
3. Cast-iron pierced cross or finial, with the head of our Saviour.
4. Cast-iron key-plate with ornamentation in bas-relief; dragon and shield charged with mailed hand and bent rapier, with the motto, "True as steel." Dragons holding ring, horse-shoe, file, and arrowhead.
5. Finial or ornament for metal-cresting, intended to be worked in wrought-iron.
6. Grille with gablet and fleur-de-lis terminal in cast-iron, with panels partially filled in with pierced iron-plate.
7. Design for cast-iron railing, the twisted bars are more suitable for wrought than cast work.

Plate 42

1. Cast-iron finial with St. George and the Dragon, shield with St. George's cross gules on argent.
2. Wrought-iron hinge, with crenated foliage.
3. Wrought-iron hinge, with eyes and wings.
4. Cast-iron hinge, shown broken for application to different lengths.
5. Cast-iron hinge with cock and motto "Vigilans; C. K. 73."
6. Cast-iron hinge, with raised edges and flowers in low-relief.
7. Bracket for gas in brass formed with pansies.
8. Bracket for gas in brass formed with fuchsias. This system, however, of making gas jets come out of flowers is not to be commended.
9. Metal corner for book cover or other purposes.
10. Key-plate, in two layers or plates of metal.
11. Ornamental head for nail.

Plate 43

1. Copper vane with fish and initials "I.E."
2 and 3. Brass corners or ornaments for wooden book covers.
4. Cast-iron staircase railing in square iron.
5. Ornamental terminals for railing in cast-iron, principal one surmounted with pelican upon ball.
6 and 7. Bosses or bolt heads.
8. Bracket for light in chased brass, with chameleon, viper, and snail.
9. Portion of cast-iron grille or railing.
10. Keyhole plate or escutcheon, with Love on the heart and armed with the key of love.
11. Wrought-iron key-plate with incised ornamentation, for alms-box, with the impaled hands and feet and wounded heart, to represent the five wounds of our Saviour.
12. Bronze handle or knocker, with head of hound.

Plate 44

1. Wrought-iron finial and copper vane, with stars and swallow.
2, 8, 9, 13, and 14. Door-handles for bronze or wrought-iron, with cut or moulded plates.
3, 10, and 11. Wrought-iron key-plates, the first with entwined dragons worked on plate.
4 and 5. Ornamental nail heads.
6 and 7. Foliated scroll work for wrought-iron or brass. Ornamentation in wrought-iron, crowned V, with rose, shamrock, and thistle.

15. Metal bow for key, which may be executed as shown or pierced.
16. Wrought-iron foliated terminal ornament.

Geometric Ornament

Plate 45

1. Eight-pointed star, for inlay in marble or wood. The lines indicate the mode of contrasting the colours, which may be black, white, red, and yellow.
2. Square form suited for glazing, inlay, or filled in with ornament, founded on a four-petalled flower.
3. Eight-petal flower-form with cross in centre. Groundwork or lines for ornamental square panel decoration.
4 and 5. Geometrical diapers for colours or glazing with tinted glass.
6. Eight-pointed star in vesica, with four divisions filled in with flamboyant lines. May be filled in with tracery or foliage.
7. Cross arrangement formed by semicircles interlaced; the angles being indicated as filled in with flower-buds. The same general form may be ornamented and varied in a number of different ways, still retaining the leading lines. The form is a very ancient one, and was much used by the early Christians. The cross vesicas, Fig. 226, was another favourite and early arrangement. Probably, in times of persecution, they were valued as being emblematical of the cross, without having an actual cross too plainly indicated.
8. Six-petal flower-form or "kite star," with spherical triangles on the hexagon, contained in a circle and square. This combination of spherical triangles, when repeated, gives the lines of what is known as the "Canterbury diaper," which is a very elegant diaper sculptured in stone in low relief on the south side of the choir. It is there filled in with six-petalled flowers and trefoils.
9. Combination of square and five circles in the form of a cross or quatrefoil, for glazing or marble inlay.
10. Interlaced guilloche bands, for diaper in low relief filled in with colour.
11. Combustion of square with double diagonal bands and crosses at the intersections for glazing. Without the crosses it forms a well-known pattern for glazing, often found in Elizabethan and other old English houses.
12. Hexafoil, containing concave-sided hexagon and six-petalled flower.
13. Trefoil intersected by the triple petals of the snowdrop. Centre for glazing in tinted glass.

Inlays, Labyrinths and Diapers

Plate 46

1. Labyrinth inlaid in marble of two colours, somewhat similar to one which existed in the church of St. Bertin at St. Omer.
2. Circular labyrinth from the nave floor of Chartres Cathedral, formed of blue and white stone inlay; other colours are also used in different parts.
3. Flaming star with coronet and date, for inlay.
4. Panel with centre cross, borders, and other portions of various designs, for geometrical inlay or parquetry.
5 and 6. Strap and geometrical inlay border.
7. Border with combinations of right-angled triangle.
8. Foliated inlay border with scalloped edges.
9. Inlay border, white and black interrupted hexagons.
10 and 11. Chinese or Japanese geometrical diapers, for painting on porcelain or for inlay. These are both formed on the triangle and hexagon.

Fig. 226

Plate 47

1. Triangular interlacing bands for diaper for parquetry or other inlay, with stars at the intersections of the white bands.

2 and 3. Variations upon the last combination, with flowers at the intersections, and cubes filling in between the triangular bands. A combination of cubes formed upon the hexagonal lines, in black, white, and gray marble, was a favourite form of pavement in the last century. It is, however, a very objectionable pattern, from its representing the cubes as if in perspective with one angle standing up,—thus losing the character that pavement should have—that of looking flat and even for walking upon.

4. Interlaced incised line, on white stone or marble filled in with black cement. Four varieties of borders, incised and filled with cement. The broader bands may be filled with cement of a different colour, or inlaid with coloured stone or marble.

5, 6, 7, and 8. Foliated diapers upon imbricated or fish-scale lines, for painting, stencilling, or wall-papers.

9 and 10. Geometrical tile pavements, on triangle, and one form fitting by reversing into each other.

11. Border of interlaced ribbon, formed by incised line, and filled in with black or coloured cement. The ground tooled in lines to give variety of surface.

12 and 13. Upright foliated and geometrical designs, for painted dados for rooms, or for executing in paper.

14. Marquetry border for woods of various colours and shades.

Plate 48

1. Incised brass filled in with black cement, the broader portions with colour. A crest formed of a mason's lewis with the motto "Hold fast," for the name "Lewis."

2. Panel for line-painted decoration, with ground filled in with colour. Continuous ribbon, with variations upon the motto "Amour par tout."

3. Panel for painted decoration upon the same motto in English, "All for love," with continuous line forming hearts and true lover's knot, filled in with shamrock foliage.

4, 5, 6, and 7. Four varieties of four-leaved diaper, with four other varieties of leaves at the sides. For painting, stencilling, or wall-paper.

8. Centre of interlaced crescents.

9. Centre containing triple arrangement of oak foliage in two colours.

10. Star and cloud diaper.

11. Diaper formed of triple gyrating cones and lines.

12. Alternating letter Z diaper.

13. Fish diaper with conventional water.

14, 15, 16, and 17. Fret and open-line diapers or filling-in, for enrichment of surface in china or porcelain.

18. Alternate-leaved bands for surface decoration. One-half of band may be also applied to metal cresting.

19. Outline fleur-de-lis, leaf, and berries, for pattern of textile fabric.

20. Acorn-and-heart enriched band for painting.

21. Stencil pattern for self-tone decoration—that is, the ornament stencilled in the same colour as the ground but darker, or *vice versa*.

Blazonry and Heraldic Ornament

Plate 49

1. A cartel for the commencement of the tournay: black and white. This example exemplifies a change which sometimes takes place in a shield of arms, termed *counterchanging*. It denotes a reciprocal exchange of metal for colour, and colour for metal, either in the same charge, or the same composition as in this instance, where sable is counterchanged with argent.

2. Faith, Hope, and Charity, with Justice and Mercy above. Faith, shield divided into light and darkness, party per fess or and sable, charged with a cross resting upon the neck of a serpent surmounted on a skull. Sin and Death overcome by the power of the cross, which has for crest the celestial crown. Supporters two angels holding the lower shields. Hope, party per fess sable and sea proper, charged with the firmly planted anchor as the last. Charity, on a shield party per pale sable and or, the pelican feeding its young with its own life blood, proper, the heart below gules, being typical of love. The term *proper* indicates the natural colour of any object.

3. Sword of state, with A, King's crown; B, Duke's coronet; C, Marquis; D, Earl; E, Viscount; and F, Baron.

4. Papal Tiara, or triple crown, cross and keys of St. Peter.

5. Austrian Imperial crown.

6. Crown of Charlemagne.

7. Crown of France. Louis le Grand (XIV.).

8. Bishop's crozier.

9. The royal sceptre of England surmounted by the orb and cross. The *orb*, a separate ball of gold six inches in diameter, upon which is placed a golden cross enriched with diamonds, pearls and other precious stones, is placed in the monarch's right hand before the coronation; and after the ceremony is borne in the left, while the *sceptre* is borne in the right.

Plate 50

1. An esquire's helmet and mantling or and sable, with crest of pelican feeding its young. The mantling or lambrequin was a small mantle attached to the helm, and hanging down over the shoulders of the wearer. It is often so adjusted as to form a background for the shield or helm, and as it was necessarily much exposed, and cut and torn in the melée, this is indicated by the jagged edges and irregular form given to mantlings by heralds. The ribbon with motto, "For the law and the people," is intermingled with the mantling.

2. Shield containing rebus upon the name "Hartwell Horn."

3. Circle with border containing horse-shoes, with emblems of rose, shamrock, and thistle, and spaces on each side filled by spurs. This is a rebus referring to the profession of the bearer, a farrier. Shield divided party per fess; in chief, a pegasus; in base, a bridle.

4. Grand seal, containing a knight "à cheval" armed cap-a-pie, trampling on the dragon, indicative of love and valour. Arms, quarterly, first and fourth, or, a lion rampant, sable; second and third, bendy, sable and azure,[1] a dove volant, argent.

5. Shield, gules, on a bend sinister, sable,[1] a flaming arrow, proper, between six flames of fire, proper. Motto, "Light in light." Crest, a lion's head, with mantling of lion's skin. Squire's helm and sword.

6. Oval panel containing the united arms of the "Queen of Hearts" and "Hope." Supporters, griffon and lion; motto, "I hope, I dare."

7. Shield, of cartouche character; party per pale or and sable, a double eagle, counterchanged.

8. Heraldic fanciful design. Smile and Frown. Shield, stars of light and darkness; party per fess argent and sable, counterchanged.

Plate 51

1. Shield emblematical of love and valour; double crest, crowned harpy and cockatrice, divided by the initial I, surmounted by heart, and interlaced with motto and true-lover's knot. Supporters, dexter, man crowned with oak foliage and armed with club; sinister, wild man armed with club.

2 and 3. Foreign coronets.

4. Arms, with collar carrying double-headed lion badge and ermine mantle, party per bend, charged with inverted orb surmounted by crowned skull. Supporters, men with terminal bodies, the dexter armed with sword, wearing portcullis, and crowned with mural crown; the sinister carrying sceptre, wearing harrow badge, and crowned with oak foliage. Disengaged arms supporting royal helmet. Crest a skull-cap.

5. Rebus: St. Andrew, with saltire cross, represented fishing. Name, "Andrew Fisher."

---

[1] Colour upon colour, which is bad heraldry. The artist has not in all cases adhered literally to the heraldic laws, but has sometimes studied, as in these cases, the good effect of his work only.

6. Armed cupid; shield charged with two fishes gyrate in water, proper.

7. Triple fish in circle on flowing gyrate form, or, gules and azure, counterchanged.

8. The initial S, with the badge of Ulster. Argent, a sinister hand,[1] couped at the wrist and erect, gules. The distinctive ensign of the order and rank of Baronets, instituted in 1612 by James I., is the ancient armorial ensign of the Irish Kingdom of Ulster.

Plate 52

1. Wolf and lamb terminating in interlaced foliage, with shield charged with wattle.

2. Knight and banneret, charged with a dragon engorging a woman. The knight supposed to be taking a vow for the destruction of the dragon, as St. George is said to have done.

3. Oval ornamentally treated, containing shield or, charged with triple lion with one head, gules. Motto, "Three in one."

4. Circular design for medal or seal. Page à cheval with lance bearing the legend "Forward," carrying a shield argent, charged with lion rampant sable, and crest, lion's head of the last. Motto, "Without fear and without reproach."

5. Circular design for seal: heraldic ship with sail argent, charged with rampant lion gules, with crest at the mast head, lion's head of the last. Angel lighting the way at the prow, and angel guiding at the helm. Motto, "Cast thy bread upon the waters, for thou shalt find it after many days."

6 and 7. Crowns of Louis XIII. and Henry IV. of France.

Plate 53

1. Royal helmet and crest for England, with ornamental mantling, and motto of the order of the Garter. "Evil be to him that evil thinks." Supported by demi-lion and unicorn, issuing out of rose and thistle.

2. Foreign coronet.[2]

3. St. George and the Dragon on fancifully formed shield.

4. Demi-rose and thistle, for England and Scotland united under one crown. Badge of the time of the union with Scotland.

5. Medal with ship, carrying banners charged with the arms of the three kingdoms, England, Ireland, and Scotland, and flag of the union at the stern. Also pennons charged with the national badges, the Rose, Shamrock, and Thistle.[3]

6. The crown of Scotland.

7. The crown of Russia.

8. Cartouche shield, azure, an anchor, argent; on a chief wavy, argent, a naval crown proper.

9. Fancifully formed shield, gules; swords in saltire, or, with triple foliage proper. On a chief embattled, or, a mural crown.

10. Trefoil in circle, containing national emblems and motto, "Three in one." The spandrels filled with dolphins.

11. Circular design or badge, the union of the Rose, Shamrock, and Thistle.

12. The royal arms of her Majesty Queen Victoria, with the supporters treated in a picturesque manner, not heraldically correct nor severe in taste.

13 and 14. Continental crowns.[2]

Plate 54

1. Arms with cupids as supporters. Shield gules, bird with wings erect gorging fish. Closed helmet with mantling and coronet. Double crest—dexter a bezant, or, and sinister a heart, gules.

2. Rebus, bell and daisy; motto, "à la belle Marguerite." Name, "Margaret Bell."

---

[1] In consequence of the drawing having been made upon the plate, the hand has not been reversed as it ought to be. The hand should be "sinister."

[2] The variety in the forms of crowns used by foreign barons during the middle ages was very great. They were not limited in their forms to indicate the special rank of the wearer, as in English heraldry.

[3] The Imperial United Standard or "Union Jack," as now used, was first displayed at the Tower of London and at Dublin Castle on 1st January, 1801. The first union flag contained the crosses of St. George and St. Andrew only, for England and Scotland. The cross of St. George is gules on a field argent; St. Andrew, a saltire argent on a field azure; and that of St. Patrick, a saltire gules on a field argent.

3. Rebus. Flower, keys, and monogram. Name, "Flora Keys."

4. Rebus. Bolt through tun and olive-tree growing out of it; monogram. Name, "Olivia Bolton."

5. Coronetted shield within circular wreath. Party per fess or and sable, charged with a lion rampant, counterchanged.

6. Shield in an antique bark, or, on a bend sable three escallop shells argent. Supporters, sea-horses on the deck, with mast and furled sail above. Paddle in lower part, with monogram.

7. Foreign crown.[1]

8. Ornamental shield, sable, diapered, charged with lion rampant with quadruple tail, argent. Dragon under shield, and halberdier on dexter side with halberd on shoulder and supporting crest, a swan with wings erect, on helmet open and in profile for nobility.

9. Mantling argent charged with serpent, gules, devouring a woman. Crest demi-woman, with arms extended, in the dexter hand a bird, and in the sinister a fish. Supported by Moors or Ethiopians with clubs.

10. Shield, gyrony of six, sable and or, in middle chief and dexter and sinister base nine trefoils, two and one, in each gyron of the first.

11. Rebus, with page supporting initial letters I.L., with legend "Light on." Name "John Leighton."

Renaissance Ornamentation

Plate 55

1. Flemish pilaster, dated 1551. This kind of scroll work is usually distinguished as cartouche work, from its resemblance to stiff rolled-up paper. It was also common in France, and it occurs very plentifully in Elizabethan. (See Plate 69.) The composition (No. 1) is made up with scroll-work and parts in perspective, all in high relief, together with fruit, serpent, vase, and grotesque figures, the whole built up upon the head of a sitting figure, and crowned with a phœnix. It is an early example of *constructed ornamentation*, a vicious system that prevailed so much in Renaissance work.

2 and 3. Semicircular heads or panels, and having partly a Gothic character. The first with vase and grotesque animals, the other with shield and radiating tracery.

4. Dryad with boy satyr, cornucopia and flowers, for stone carving in high relief.

5. Faun and satyr with accompaniments to pair with the last. Mythological figures were frequently introduced in the Renaissance.

6. Panel containing angel with shields charged with cross and cross-keys and crowned harpy.

Plate 56

1. Shield within horse-shoe, party per pale, argent and gules, two hearts counterchanged with the field. On a chief, sable, two mullets, argent and gules. Crest, flame of fire surrounded by chain, proper. Supported by grotesque dragons.

2. Sculpture for tympanum of doorway or semicircular panel. Head of river-god, surmounted by compass, supported by two sitting female figures holding rudder and paddle. Ground of gold stars on blue.

3. Panel with eccentric combination of grotesque animals, birds, scorpion, snail, &c.

4. Tail-piece for painting, wall decoration. Cartouche shield with the monogram "C. O. G.," surmounted by satyr's head, supported by scroll cupids and birds carrying festoons of flowers.

5. Bracket or hook in metal formed of winged monster with female head wearing cap of liberty.

6. Date label, surrounded by foliated serpents and cartouche work.

7. Shield containing the French cypher, double L, helmet and scroll mantling. Crest, winged mailed arm carrying porte-crayon. Lower portion made up with open book, and terminal of cat's head and rat.

Plate 57

1. Oval panel or shield supported by winged figure carrying the sword of justice. Above, cupid with torch; below, head supporting vase, flanked by boy and branch, with fruit, &c.
2. Half panel with Minerva and shield, with centres of heads and vase, flanked by birds, festoons and scroll work above, and cupid with torch below.
3 and 4. Wheat and rose, for raised and chased metal finger-plates for doors.
5. Grotesque mask. These were of constant occurrence in this style.
6. Bas-relief panel, containing cartouche inclosing burning heart engraved with tazza, flanked by male and female satyrs holding in their hands the thyrsus of Bacchus and supporting cupids.

Plate 58

1 and 2. Flat carved terminals out of the surface. Busts of king and queen, crowned with foliated hair, beard, &c.
3 and 4. String-courses carved in relief, arranged on alternating inclined planes and repetition of similar forms.
5. Arabesque panel, for painting, or sculpture in low relief, with foliated figures, heads, and dolphins. The lower portion filled with the pelican feeding its young with its own blood.
6 and 7. Panels with foliated scroll borders, suitable for niello or buhl work.
8. Ornamental vase for execution in silver.
9. Square flower for panel.
10. Design for foliated inlay or incised work.

Plate 59

1. Sculptured pedestal with centre panel containing folded linen, flanked by male and female sitting figures, with festoons of flowers. Cupids and crowned head in frieze above; satyr's head, swans and sculptured water below. This example, as also 4 and 5, Plate 55, are intended to show that intimate admixture of sculpture and ornament which was so prevalent and characteristic of this period.
2. Venus and dolphins, with an arrangement of ribbons carrying medallions containing portraits of artists of the period.
3. Ornamental fleur-de-lis composed of foliage and berries.
4. Terminal monster for bracket.
5. Panel containing an ornamental combination of male and female satyrs and fauns, with festoons and foliage.

Plate 60

1. Mermaid and dolphins in lunette or semi-circular panel for painting.
2 and 3. Terminal heads or arm-rests for stalls or chairs, for carving in wood-work.
4. Arabesque panel in flat relief, with gold ground and blue grounds in centre. Subject: Night. A female figure about to envelop herself in her veil; the evening-star above; triple interlaced crescents below, the device of the celebrated Diana of Poitiers, with sleeping cat, and mice at play. The minor arabesque subjects are, boys with candles, sleeping masks, bat with star, incense vases, roosting peacocks, flowers, and scroll work.
5. Grotesque combination of snake entangled and mixed up with legs and arms.
6. Contest between a dwarf and a dragon.
7. Heraldic composition: shield or, charged with dragon sable, surmounted by open helmet, feather crest, with foliated mantling sword and belt.
8. Decorative vase with flowers, and scroll encircling the vase formed of the lily.
9. Cartouche with winged head and interlacing bird scrolls.

Plate 61

1. Tympanum for segmental-headed doorway carved in alto-relievo. Armorial bearings as for a seaport town. Shield argent, charged with lion rampant, gules; crest, lion's head of the last; on closed helmet with mantling. Supporters, sea god and goddess, carrying oar with trident and spear. Angles filled in with dragons strangling snakes.

2 and 3. Centre flowers for carving.
4 and 5. Scroll terminals, female figure and cupid; winged head and bell.
6. Spear piercing entwined serpent with foliage.
7. Entwined double-headed serpent in vesica.
8. Mask and scroll foliage.

Plate 62

1. Ornamental scroll figure bearing flower-baskets, for execution in flat relief and decorated in gold and colour.
2. Lioness-head claw or leg for pedestal, with entwined skin.
3. Bracket; head of satyr with vine and other foliage.
4. Composition for inlay. Vase, out of which spring conventional scroll foliage and flowers. Monogram "A. D." in lower compartment.
5, 6, and 9. Masks for sculpture.
7. Spandrel filling in between circular panels. Boys and bust in centre with monogram "B. A. B." below, surrounded with foliage and ram's head.
8. Spandrel between circular panels with imbricated frames. Angel scroll bearing grapes and vase supported by a bearded-lion altar. The scroll issuing from the angel terminating in rose and leaves, with cock's head and rabbit.

Plate 63

1. Composition for centre of panel, with centaur on shield surrounded by masks and foliage.
2. Kneeling supporter. Chained negress and scroll work.
3. Fish and scroll of sea-weed and shell.
4. Female kneeling figure with mural crown, leaning on shield, charged with arms.
5. Demi-shield with kneeling female supporter.
6. Rebus, I (eye) L, with olive branch. Name, "John Leighton."
7. Frame for glass (containing ornamental vase). Group of children above, bearing palette, compasses and brush, and mask in centre. Below boys carrying maul-stick and plumb-rule, with festoon of curtain looped up to animal's head in centre.
8. Fanciful arrangement of winged harpy, with boy scroll and butterfly; to flank a medallion or shield in the centre, a small portion of which is shown.
9. Composition for execution in statuary marble. Angels with scroll terminal bodies supporting a celestial crown, and a mantle bearing the representation of a skull in a sacred chalice and covered by the red hat and insignia of a cardinal.

Plate 64 (Superficial)

1. Geometrical diaper, filled in with crowned rose rising out of fleur-de-lis. The other compartments having shamrock, thistle, and oak issuing from fleurs-de-lis.
2, 3, 7, and 8. Ornamental circles.
4 and 5. Interlaced bands for parquetry.
6. Frieze of alternated heart-forms filled with delicate scroll-work.
9. Central triple flower arrangement, alternating with centres containing strawberries.
10. Ogee net-work tracery, alternating with lower form of the same character.
11. Diaper of conventional foliated forms.

Plate 65 (Superficial)

1. Conventional wall decoration of fabric pattern.
2. Cross with half circles interlaced.
3. Centre with half circles interlaced having split points, alternating with four flower calices.
4. Interlaced double triangles in a circle and a flower of six petals in the centre.
5. Four vesicas interlaced in a circle with fleur-de-lis and leafage.
6. Ornamentally arranged fleur-de-lis, with black drop ornaments and scrolls.
7. Octofoil with heart-form cross and black foliage.
8. Octofoil containing banded and interlaced cross, with alternating and interlaced bands and foliage.

9. Centre for fabric pattern with geometrical bands, ivy-leaf, and other foliage.
10 and 11. Square quatrefoils filled in with snow-drop and triple foliage.

Plate 66 (Superficial)
1. Diamond and oblong interlaced enrichment for textile fabric.
2. Textile fabric, leaf and pansy.
3. Textile fabric, conventional foliage.
4. Fern fronds in diagonal cross and interlaced geometrical form in the centre. Below, a composition of lines and circles filled in with foliage.
5. Interlaced tinted and black form with triple terminations, and centres filled with leafage.
6. Interlaced square and flowing bands with ogee quatrefoil centre and foliated ground for carpet or mat.

Plate 67 (Superficial)
1. Geometrical pattern of circles and square in interlaced bands filled in with pointed quatrefoil and foliage.
2. Square and diagonal cross centre in black for repetition in wall diaper, and filled in with black and white triple-berry foliage, on tinted ground; the dotted ground being in gold.
3. Geometrical interlaced double quatrefoils and circles in white and chocolate on tinted ground.
4. Strapwork, interlaced form with ivy and trefoil foliage, for marquetry.
5. Interlaced strapwork panel and oblong label in the centre with foliage, for engraving on metal, the black bands being filled in with coloured cement.

Plate 68 (Superficial)
1. Diagonal bands for wall diaper. White on chocolate and gray on white.
2. A similarly treated diaper, formed with interlaced monograms, "D. W."
3. Ornamental painted fluting, for repetition in a hollow or cavetto.
4. Foliated circle or boss with dogs in the centre running round ball-flower.
5. Diapered diamond centre, with foliated angles and arrow-headed leaf and interlaced line scrolls.
6 and 7. Patterns for lace work.
8 and 9. Panels of arabesque and interlaced strapwork.
10. Woven fabric; mat or rug. Diamond, circle and interlaced strapwork, picked out in colours and set in dark neutral-tinted ground.

English Renaissance Ornamentation

Plate 69 (Elizabethan and Jacobean)
1. Angle strap ornament with conventional strap, scroll, and mono-gram "W. S." This kind of ornamentation was often executed in plaster or stucco on ceilings or walls.
2. Bolt and scroll with cartouche shield containing initials "E. R." tied together with cord, the ornament forming one-half of oblong frieze enrichment executed in oak, with shield gilded.
3. Bolt and strap oval central ornament, with cartouche work and shield at bottom charged with cross spurs. Arabesque line enrich-ment or niello-work in the centre.
4. Cartouche shield within a diamond form, with the device of a falcon on a crescent tearing or killing a rat. Star, shell, and cross arrows. Date, "1551." Time of Edward VI.
5. Hanging cartouche scroll-work, with ribbons and label from a ring in lion's mouth. Surmounted by an exploding fire-ball.
6. Bolt and strap device for stucco, with cupids and motto. Bust of queen, masks, &c., with festooned drapery and looped-up cords.

Plate 70 (Elizabethan and Jacobean)
1. Square with tapering pilasters or terminals and cartouche scroll-work. Shield containing monogram "C. C. I."

2. Cartouche shield, with flowers within a grate.
3. Cartouche shield, with arabesque ornament in the centre inlaid in two colours.
4. Small heraldic monument of the Jacobean period. Shield, or; on a bend, sable, three hearts, argent; between two dexter hands, gules. Crest, a hand holding a flaming heart, placed on a closed knight's helmet from which issues an elaborate foliated mantling. Motto, "Labour and Love." The frame, which has knee corners, is surmounted by a segmental broken pediment, filled in with crowned and winged sprite.
5. Rustic pole for long panel or pilaster, with ribbon, foliage, and hanging shield; charged with monogram "G. A." on sable ground.
6. Bolt and cartouche ornament for frieze on one side of centre shield or other enrichment. Central mask with interlacing circle, with nail-heads and diagonal terminal ornaments.
7. Central ornament, flat relief in alabaster on black marble, bolt and scroll with dolphins. Shield containing the arms of Shakspere, or; on a bend sable, a spear of the first. Initials and date of Shaks-pere's birth.
8. Small niche of cartouche scroll-work, entwined with rope, con-taining the subject in high relief of the "Lion in Love." Above, as a terminal ornament, is the burning heart and inter-lacing rope.
9. Ornament of bolt and square band work, with diagonal band interlaced and tying same on to centre enrichment.

French Renaissance Ornamentation

Plate 71
1. Arms of the "Grand Monarque" Louis XIV. arranged for the tympanum of a doorway. Azure; three fleurs-de-lis, or. Figures representing Fame, History, and Love, which is quite in character with the pretentious and grandiloquent manner of the time.
2, 3. Spandrels for engraving on metal work or for inlay. These give the character of many of the confused lines of scroll work of the period, called buhl-work.
4. Scroll grotesque mask.
5. Scroll and stalactite frame containing a portrait of the "Grand Monarque." The general form shows how beauty of outline is lost, and nothing gained but showy elaboration.
6. Mermaid and mask of river-god, with dolphin, shell, and rock work. The bad construction of this most vicious style is clearly apparent in this example.
7. Stalactite, shell, and rustic interlaced drop corner, for picture or glass frame.
8. Mask and dragon with scroll-work for upper part of leg to gilded console table. Period, late in the reign of Louis XIV.
9. Ditto, with draped mask. The legs for tables or other objects were never made straight in this style.

Plate 72
1. Centre portion of frieze of cornice with shepherd and dog. A great affectation of playing at shepherds and shepherdesses existed in the reign of Louis XV., and sculpture and paintings introducing Arcadian life and scenes were of frequent occurrence.
2. Scroll with sitting figure of Justice resting on the fasces.
3. Conventional Rococo scroll with lattice, vine, and dragon, showing the combination of C scrolls and rock work. Metal vase or flagon in the centre.
4. Half of centre ornament for bottom of frame or panel, with lion's head and scroll-work. Lattice and fruit. This was the character of the gilded panelling inclosing paintings, silk, or glass, so often adopted in French room decoration of the Louis XV. period.
5. Keystone of decorative arch, carrying fire-vase, cupid, bee-hive, flowers, stalactites, bulrushes, &c., with festoon and drop from keystone.
6. Scroll with satyr's head and fruit inclosing female head.
7. This figure is nearly an exact copy of a French example, and serves to show the vice in the compositions of the time. It is a caricature upon the Egyptian, being a sphinx dressed à-la-mode, and holding a fan. In the centre an ordinary dressing-glass, initial, and crown above. The background formed by pyramid.

Plate 73

1. Angle scroll for frame, Louis XV. style.
2. Composition of natural fruit and flowers issuing from shell or scroll. The mixture of the natural and artificial is seldom successful. One is too strictly copied from nature, while the other is bad in form, the main endeavour appearing to be to get rid of straight lines.
3. Scroll with cupid dressed *à-la-militaire*. Conceits of this kind were of common occurrence.
4. Shell containing cupid, Venus or mermaid, and dolphin, with shell finial, coral, water, &c.
5. Oval shield, arms of France—azure; three fleurs-de-lis, or; surrounded with shells and scroll work and stalactite drops.
6. A later and better example of flat-panel decoration in low-relief, and may be considered as an example of Louis XVI. work, although not entirely free from the vicious lines of the Rococo. An elegantly formed vase in the centre, and a partial return to straight lines in the work behind.
7. Portion of frame or shield with cockle-shell and scroll work.
8. Upper portion of a gilded support for a cut-out and shaped console table, Louis XV. period. The extent to which the tops of tables and other works were shaped was something ridiculous. It would appear as if the main idea of beauty was to avoid the straight line. Furniture was often termed *bombé* work from the constantly occurring curves of surface.

Floral Ornamentation

Plate 74

1. A composition of Rose, Corn-flower, Wheat, and Holly.
2. The Teazle arranged symmetrically for carving in low relief.
3. *Tropæolum speciosum*, arranged for painting, the flower being laid out symmetrically.
4. Fancy floret, with serrated leaves in two colours.
5. The Poppy, with seed-pods arranged ornamentally.
6. Flower with radiating leaves surrounding the stalks after the manner of Goose-grass.
7. Heath-like sprig.
8. Water-lily and Eel.
9. Conventionalized flower of the Knapweed for carving.

Plate 75

1. Arrangement of the Fuchsia for painting. Centre of panel or other decoration.
2. Scroll of berries and curled leaves.
3. Bindweed growing out of and entwining rustic pole.
4. The Thistle arranged ornamentally, for carving in low relief, out of the surface. The ground being left standing level with the highest portion of the carving. Technically known as cavo-relievo.
5 and 6. Flower sprig and grasses arranged ornamentally.
7. The Lily, arranged symmetrically and growing from combined hearts, as an emblem of purity.
8. Ivy for painting or stamped work, for book covers.
9. Plant with seeds, called the "Pope's Money." Curved stems embracing leaf.

Plate 76

1. Outline foliated forms, spirals and leaves.
2. Stick and scroll forms with flowers and berries. Root entwined ornamentally.
3. Symmetrically arranged tulip-like flowers and leaves growing from bulb with ornamental root.
4. Founded on Hyacinth growing in glass with ornamentally arranged root.
5. Hanging basket with arrangement of flowers.
6. Symmetrical arrangement of the Catch-fly.
7. The Pink, ornamentally treated.
8. Spirally arranged flower growing from stick.
9. The Pomegranate and Poppy for painting in a panel.
10. Currant leaves and hanging berries entwined spirally.
11. *Equisetum* or Horse-tail, with ornamental accompaniments formed of the seeds of the Shepherd's Purse.

12 and 13. Hanging and scrolled florets.
14. Open pea-pods and tendrils, for painting on a dark ground.

Plate 77

1. The Maple with seed-vessels arranged symmetrically.
2. Flower with bulbous roots, scroll stems, and ivy-form leaves.
3. Group of outline sprigs for painting: Hemlock, &c.
4. Tubular flower with plaited leaf.
5. Opening leaves or bud-form. Many valuable suggestions may be obtained by observing plants while expanding their leaves and flowers.
6. Central leaf-bud with partially opened leaves, springing from plant-form.
7. Arrangement of scrolled leafage with pine or seed, for carving in low relief.
8. Maize ornamentally treated for carving.
9. Ivy-leaves arranged on a fig-leaf for painting.

Plate 78

1. Conventional flower and leafage.
2. St. John's Wort, with pinnate leaves and ornamental root.
3. Leafage and flowers conventionalized for painting
4 and 5. Polyanthus arranged as centres for painting on panels.
6. Tulip conventionalized.
7. Orchid treated symmetrically for painting or flat carving.
8. Leaves arranged upon leaves for colour or woven fabric.
9 and 10. Foliated scrolls.
11. Seven-lobed leaf with raised eyes and split interlaced stem for carving out of surface.
12. Horse-chestnut leaves on Ivy, and—
13. Maple on Ivy: symmetrical sprigs for centres or diapers.

Plate 79

1. Acorns and Oak with leaf-galls and ornamental root for carving.
2. Conventional scroll and fruit for painting or illumination.
3. Leaves of Tormentilla and conventional flowers for painting.
4. Bulbous plant (Leek) with seeds and scrolled root, arranged for carving out of the surface with raised ground in cavo-relievo.
5. Vine scroll, with grapes and tendrils ornamentally treated.
6. Scroll of heart-form leaves and flower for painting.
7. Sprig of Raspberry.
8. Foliated cross for gold and colour.
9. Fruit sprig.
10. Scroll of Passion-flower entwining stick.
11. Strawberry sprig, with simplified leaves.
12. Leaf upon leaf with enlaced stem. White upon gold.

Plate 80

1. Grass-form plant with seeds, arranged symmetrically for carving in panel.
2. Fir-cone and conventional leafage.
3. Sprig with radiating leaves. The two halves varied.
4. Scroll of Fuchsia, growing from stick.
5. Arum.
6. Honeysuckle and trefoil leaves.
7. Scroll sprig—Lily.
8. Arrangement of common garden pea, with leafage and tendrils, carved out of the surface. The tendrils on the ground incised in double lines.
9, 10, 11, 12. Ornamental sprigs.
13. Frieze-panel of oak and acorns for stone carving, the light and shade of the leaves being increased by leaf-galls.

Plate 81

1. Central sprig with seeds of Pomegranates.
2 and 3. Sprigs arranged from nature for painted decoration.
4 and 5. Foliated forms for carving.
6. Dock leaves and Hart's-tongue fern, arranged for carving out of the surface, and decorated by gold and colour.
7 and 8. Sprigs.
9. Geometrically arranged sprig with plaited leaves.
10. Strawberry plant with fruit and flowers.

11. Ferns, Grass, and May-fly ornamentally treated. Opening fronds of Hard-fern and Polypody.

12. Symmetrically arranged flower-sprig for decoration or woven fabric. Wild Sage.

13. Conventional Rose for black-and-gold decoration.

Plate 82 (Miscellaneous)

The designs on the following Plates are arranged for various decorative purposes: in the flat for painting, inlay, or carving; in the form of centres, borders, or for the enrichment of surfaces. Many of the examples may also be applied to other purposes, such as encaustic tiles, stained glass, stamped leather-work, paper-hangings, calico-printing, and also to the ornamentation of the products of the loom and the printing-press.

1. Upright border or panel of double flowing wave-line, interlaced with broken line, and filled in with Ivy and other foliage. For painted decoration.

2. Conventional triangular centre figure with foliage, for marble or other inlay.

3. Symmetrical palm-leaf flower on eight-pointed irregular star-form, for wood inlay.

4. Upright and alternately inverted flower border, for woven fabric.

5. Bindweed leaf pattern upright border growing on ribbon. Painted decoration.

6. Border carved in low relief. Ivy with interrupted central stem and curved branches set out upon interlacing vesicas.

7. Interlaced geometrical form on diagonal square filled in with Ivy leaves and berries.

8. Cruciform arrangement of flowers in a pointed quatrefoil.

9. Symmetrical flower growing from a whorl of eight leaves, for painted arched panel.

10. Cruciform treatment of the Passionflower, for mosaic inlay with gold ground. The leaves, flower, and buds being bordered with a white line.

11. Moresque forms alternating with a diagonal arrangement of fig-leaves on a gold ground.

Plate 83 (Miscellaneous)

1. Flowing scroll border with buds and flowers.

2. Triangled trefoil filled in with flowing foliage.

3. Curved hexagonal star in a circle with interlacing lines and filled in with foliage.

4. Pansy, flower and leaf border for woven fabric or decoration on gold ground.

5. Leaf and twig border with berries, for calico or other printed work. Ivy-leaved Toad-flax.

6. Horse-chestnut border for coloured decoration.

7. Upright flowing border.

8. Symmetrical ornament for border or other purposes.

9. White and black alternating leaf border growing from wave-line stem.

10. Holly scroll border with berries, for decoration on a gold ground.

11 and 12. Upright arranged geometrically formed borders filled in with flowers, for decoration or inlay.

13. Lemon plant with flowers and fruit, for chintz pattern or other printed decoration.

14. Bell-flower border, in upright divisions.

15. Border, upright divisions of flowers, alternating with mushrooms and five-pointed stars, for decoration on gold ground.

Plate 84 (Miscellaneous)

1. Interlacing circles and square, on a quatre-foil filled in with heart-form leaf foliage. For inlay.

2 and 3. Borders for inlay or decoration.

4 and 5. Diamond panels filled in with geometrical lines and foliage, for stamped leather or other purposes.

6. Geometrically arranged flowing diaper, filled in with foliated and eight-pointed star forms. For carpet.

7. Circle divided into curved triangular compartments and filled in with acorns, &c.

8. Hexagonal arrangement curved triangles filled in with ivy leaves and star centre, for inlay.

9. Diaper formed by squares with interlaced diagonal lines, filled in with four-petalled flower in the centre and fir-cones placed diagonally. Other divisions filled in with crosses and eight-petalled flowers at the angles. Encaustic tiles.

10. Flowing scroll, flower, and leaf border for decoration.

11. Geometrical border for tiles or inlay.

12. Zigzag alternating flower border, for painted decoration or paper-hanging.

13. Upright acorn border alternating with bud.

14. Leaf-form border for decoration or incised work.

Figures, Animals, Chimeras, and Trophies

Plate 85 (Figures)

1. Design for clock panel, with dial of twenty-four hours and allegorical figures of Day and Night.

2, 3, 4, 5. Decorative panel paintings of Morning (sunrise and cock-crow), Noon (the midday meal), Evening (twilight and repose from labour), Night (sleep and rest). A certain amount of poetical feeling and the adoption of conventional forms are necessary in the treatment of commonplace subjects for decoration.

Plate 86 (Figures)

1. The consolation of the cross, by the side of which springs the lily as the emblem of purity. Babe being borne to heaven in the arms of an angel.

2. The guardian angel guiding Innocence through the slough of despond: Evil being subdued and their footsteps being sustained by the cross.

3. Satan reposing, with the emblems of war and strife hung up and at rest. The branch full of thorns but devoid of leaves or fruit.

4. Finial for spire or pinnacle, formed by the angel of the resurrection listening for the signal to sound the trumpet.

5. Mercury, for a finial or vane.

6. Finial, for a spire. The avenging angel.

Plate 87 (Figures)

1. Panel containing within a triangle the nymph of love between fire and water. Attendant figures holding medallions, filled with the phœnix rising from its own ashes and the pelican feeding its young with its blood.

2. Sprite and spider, with web on a conventional tree.

3. Sprite and snail, with conventional foliage.

4. Decorative painted panel. Lovers transfixed by the dart from the bow of Cupid. Rose and lily foliage. Arcadian treatment.

5. Night. Fairy issuing out of a lily sprinkling dew over the earth.

6. Morning. Child awakening, and lark in the heavens singing to welcome the rising sun.

7. Border. Greyhound and hare in fern; bird rising, and snake escaping in the grass.

Plate 88 (Figures)

1. The wagon of Love, within the magnet of Love, which has a power over all, typified by the form of the horse-shoe.

2. War. Profitless glory leading only to death, as indicated upon the shield.

3. Peace; leading to rest, happiness, and plenty. The shield of repose emblazoned with the dove and olive-branch.

4. Agriculture. Sculptural panel for bas-relief.

5 and 6. Scroll masks in profile.

7. Babe starting on the perilous voyage of life, being deposited in the ark by an angel.

8. Allegorical head. The smiling earth teeming with life and industry.

9. Butterflies and female mask.

10. Work. Shield on a box, charged with eye and hand, and the motto "Travail," *Work*. The box bound with iron and dove-tailed, the work of the smith and carpenter, who are represented in the side compartments.

11. Sport. Boys riding a race, for painting in monotone.

Plate 89 (Figures)

1. Double female head: Wisdom and Folly. Torch entwined by serpent for wisdom, and two moths approaching the flame of the torch indicative of folly.
2. Halberdier. Bronze figure for supporting a lamp, for the newel of a staircase.
3. Plant form, with Beauty issuing from the flowers.
4. Bracket, formed of a female bust.
5. Emblem of love. The rose and lily embracing.
6. Arabesque panel in black and white, emblematical of love and fancy.
7. Animal contrast.
8. Pilgrims of love, with the heart yet untouched. Decorative frieze for painting.
9. Cupid's target, with the heart wounded and pierced by love's dart. To pair with the last.

Plate 90 (Figures)

1. Female terminal or antefixal ornament.
2. Bread and wine, arranged symbolically.
3. Musical plant, indicative of the harmony of nature.
4. Satyr with wine fountain, surrounded by the foliage of the vine.
5 and 6. Medallions, containing male and female heads, for sculpture or painting.
7. Birth of Venus, who is supposed to have sprung from the foam of the sea.
8. Ceres, with horn of plenty.
9. Venus migrating.
10. Will-o'-the-wisp, or the fairy of the night pool.

Plate 91 (Figures)

1. Sport. Ornamental decorative panel, painted on gold ground.
2 and 3. Snowdrop and Rosebud. Might be applied as carved arm-rests for chairs or stalls.
4. Composition emblematical of the ocean.
5. Love swung by Cupid in a bower of roses. Centre for panel decoration.
6. Muse with lyre, for sculpture. Supporting figure on one side of shield.
7 and 8. Ornamental centres for panels. Sage being instructed by water-sprite, and the midnight tale, *tête-à-tête.*

Plate 92 (Figures)

1. Masks of Tragedy and Comedy. Ornamental spandrel for placing between arches, with vine foliage, &c.
2 and 3. Medallions containing male and female heads—Youth and Age.
4 and 5. Figures for supporting lamps.
6 and 7. Sun and moon. Decorative centres.
8. Triple shell trefoil panel.
9. Cupids and goat, with ivy-leaf scroll. Border for decoration.
10. Bracket. Pink of Love.
11. Bracket. Cupid reposing.
12. Wine, with scroll of vine foliage. Decorative border or frieze.

Plate 93 Animals (Centres)

1. Trefoil for inlay. Triply united bats.
2. Circle containing running hares united by the ears, forming a triangle. The arms of the Isle of Man consist of three legs following each other after the same manner.
3. Triply-united foxes, with fowls and nests.
4. Triangular combination of dragon-flies, for inlay or flat sculpture.
5. Three dog's-heads united.
6. Pentagonal bird centre.
7. Triply-united cranes with interlaced wings, after the manner of Celtic ornamentation. For sculpture in low relief.
8. Circle containing a triangular combination of fish. For painted decoration.

9. Centre for decorative panel. Pentagonal arrangement of cranes and snakes.
10. Three skates in a whirlpool.
11. Hexagonal combination of three pelicans and three fishes. Centre for inlay.

Plate 94 (Animals)

1. Pelican and eel among bulrushes. For painted decoration.
2. Arrangement of bulrushes, eel, toad, dragon-flies, &c.
3. Foliage with birds and nests. Naturalesque treatment for printed fabric.
4. Border with a conventional representation of water, out of which grow the water-lily and bulrushes, alternating with dragon-flies. Printed border for woven fabric or earthenware.
5. Panel for painting or mosaic inlay with gold ground. Foliated scroll in colour with pheasant and fox-head centre.
6. Composition of swan, fish, arum, and bulrushes.
7. United flamingos on a fish.
8. Snail and star border, for porcelain decoration.
9. Ornamentation for printed or woven fabric. Grass stem and seeds, with caterpillar, chrysalis, and butterfly, on foliated ground.

Plate 95 (Chimeras)

1. Dragon and pine. Sculpture in bas-relief.
2. Toad-stool and snake, with head of Despair flanked by nondescript imps. For carving.
3. Mirth and Melancholy, or Tragedy and Comedy, under the wings of a harpy. Carved head over doorway in alto-relievo.
4. Dolphins devouring human bodies. Composition for pedestal.
5. Monogram and chimerical figure.
6. Grasshopper-bird dragons, symmetrically arranged with foliage. For carving out of surface.
7. Poppy and bats with moon, indicative of sleep. For printed chintz.
8. Border for decoration. Fight among nondescript dragons.

Plate 96 (Trophies, &c.)

1. Wine, with scroll of vine.
2. Beer, with hop and barley growing out of barrel.
3. Tobacco, growing out of pipe. These are for painting or carving in low relief.
4. Fish. Net and shell with trident, &c.
5. Fowl. Turkey, goose, and cock, surmounted by feathers and dish, with motto.
6. Flesh. Beef, mutton, pork, venison, and hare, with spear and bow, the whole surmounted by a boiling pot upon the fire.

These three last trophies are for carving on panels of dining-room buffet.

Letters and Monograms

Plate 97

1, 2, 3, 4. Letters B, O, E, A, ornamented after the manner of various manuscripts.
5. Shield containing the sacred monogram I. H. S. on a red cross.
6. Initial letter I, in the Celtic or Irish style.
7. Letter G, enriched with foliage and ribbon.
8. Cross with crown of thorns and I. H. S.
9. Letter H, formed with rope and interlaced with foliage.
10. Initial letter A, Irish or Anglo-Saxon.
11. Rustic letter S on wood work.
12. Crest, locomotive engine rampant.
13. Letter W in relief in panel.
14. Shield with letters A. D. J.
15. Letter N, interlaced lines.
16. Letter S formed with ribbon and foliage.
17. Shield containing monogram J. K. C.
18. Strap or ribbon letter N.
19. Letter Y inlaid with foliage.

Plate 98

1. Monogram B. G. on a shield.
2. Letter S with interlaced lines.
3. Letter Q filled in with lilies on ground divided into gold and blue.
4. Monogram V. A on a shield with oak foliage.
5. Letter M.
6. Hollow initial letter I interlaced with narwhal on wave ground.
7. Letter K, enriched with foliage and flowers.
8. Initial word As.
9. Letter F with sportsman and owl entwined by foliage.
10. Illuminated letter O.
11. Letter W, monk and wine in a cellar, with vine foliage.
12. Letter R, with strawberry.
13. Monogram O. E, with hart and dart.
14. Letter Z, zany with sun-flowers.
15. Letter K, formed with oak branches and acorns.
16. Monogram B. E. I.
17. Monogram I. A. on shield.
18. Monogram T. R on a leaf.
19. Monogram on a shield, J. P. N.
20. Monogram I. S.

Miscellaneous

Plate 99

1. Angel issuing from the sun, the emblem of light, with entwined ribbon or scroll, containing the motto, *Son art en Dieu*, "His art is from God."
2. Griffin support for a pedestal. For carving in stone.
3. Sitting leopard: support or bracket for a console table.
4. Panel containing a shield charged with an ancient ship with a sail, having, on a canton, a fleur-de-lis (arms of Paris). The shield hung on a conventional oak-tree, bearing acorns and leaves with leaf-galls.
5. Jupiter typified by the eagle, grasping the thunderbolt and fed by cupid. Composition for painting.
6. Ornamental central form, suggesting an animal's head with horns. For inlay.
7. Leaf-sprig with cupids disturbing a nest of young birds.
8. Ivy-buds treated symmetrically.
9. Lunette for painting, containing the head of an ancient soldier, with leather casque and *couvrenuque*, on a decorated ground.
10. Triangular fret for ornamental band.
11. Band or frieze formed of flowing triple leaves, on plain leaf-forms.

Plate 100

1. Ribbon star or centre interlaced with scroll work of two kinds.
2. The passion-flower treated symmetrically.
3. Ornamental shield, with arrow. Sable, and chief or. The whole surmounted by the interlaced double L, for Louis or Lewis.
4. Scroll foliage and flowers arranged geometrically and counter-changed for inlay.
5. Eccentrically formed panel containing an arrangement of the pansy and spiral seed-vessels. The centre flower charged with the shamrock and fleur-de-lis.
6. Irregular hexagonal panel with interlaced foliage.
7. Circle divided hexagonally by flowing wheel-like curves, filled with scroll foliage counterchanged.
8. One division of an ornamental cresting for engraving on metal.
9. Symmetrical arrangement of rose and round-lobed foliage for the centre of a panel.
10. Foliated and scrolled centre for carving in cavo-relievo.
11. Frieze enrichment divided by diagonal squares, and interlaced by eccentrically designed foliage.

12. A variation upon the Moorish fret as given at Fig. 168.

Plate 101

1. Ornamental squares for painted diaper work, or to be used alternately for a string-course or band.
2. Palette charged with the initial P in interlaced lines, with foliage, maul-stick, and brushes.
3. Ornamental mask. Old Age.
4. Raffaelesque painting for pilaster or panel.
5. Date-plate with the monogram "I. L."
6. Ornamental cross for metal work.
7. Harp-formed bracket, consisting of a female bust terminating in an animal's claw.
8. A bronze vase-shaped tripod lamp, entwined by a serpent.
9. Diaper for a dado for painting or wallpaper.
10. Triangularly divided border filled in with foliage.
11. A supporting dolphin for a pedestal.
12. A bracket or support formed by a combination of foliage and the leg of a lion.

FRONTISPIECE

1. Centre. The artist and artisan having produced a vase or cup, which has been suggested by the form of the lily, are comparing it with the plant—both having been influenced by the same feeling or mutual understanding, as indicated by the union of the hands in the window above.
2. Geometry. The compass, with a flower and a newt (plant and animal life). The circle divided into semicircle and quadrant. The circle containing the double triangle or hexagonal star. The circle with the square and octagon. These primary figures when united to the curves found in plant and animal life are the basis of all beautiful forms in art.
3. The star and ivy diaper—suggested by viewing external nature through the casement.
4. Conventionalism necessary in the highest art—as shown by the antique and mediæval modes of rendering the lily and the honey-suckle.
5. Opposite forms united by art—beauty of one kind blended with that of another, as that of the fish with the human female form.
6. Symmetrical imitative representations for decoration or orna-ment should be taken directly from nature.
7. The infinity of form, as exhibited in twenty-four varieties of natural leaves.
8, 9, 10, 11. The architecture of all ages, as represented by columns.
8. The Egyptian (2000 B.C.) majestic, massive, and enduring. Conventionalized from the papyrus plant. 9. The Assyrian (900 B.C.) as exemplified by one of the columns from Persepolis (de-stroyed 300 B.C.), and supposed to be similar to those which supported the upper stories of the palaces at Nimroud and Khorsabâd. It bears an affinity to the Indian columns with bracket capitals, and was the precursor of the Greek Ionic. 10. Grecian Ionic from the Erechtheum at Athens (400 B.C.). The Doric, how-ever, is more characteristic of Athenian art, as seen in the Par-thenon; but the Ionic is considered coeval with the Doric, and was much used at an early period in the Grecian states of Asia Minor. 11. The Gothic, the type of the mediæval art of Europe (A.D. 1200). The column consisted of small shafts clustered round a centre core, and was not limited to height as in the antique examples. The columns supported pointed arches, and the main lines of Gothic architecture were vertical, with great height and extreme lightness of construction. The columns of antiquity, usually distinguished as classic, carried horizontal beams, producing solidity and grandeur without extreme height.